THE MARSHALL CAVENDISH
☆ ☆ ☆ ILLUSTRATED ☆ ☆ ☆
ENCYCLOPEDIA OF
WORLD WAR II

VOLUME 12

THE MARSHALL CAVENDISH
☆ ☆ ☆ ILLUSTRATED ☆ ☆ ☆
ENCYCLOPEDIA OF
WORLD WAR II

Based on the original text by
Lieutenant Colonel Eddy Bauer

CONSULTANT EDITOR

Brigadier General James L. Collins, Jr., U.S.A.
CHIEF OF MILITARY HISTORY, DEPARTMENT OF THE ARMY

MARSHALL CAVENDISH CORPORATION/NEW YORK

CONTENTS

Editorial Director: Brian Innes
Editor-in-chief; Brigadier Peter Young, D.S.O., M.C., M.A.
Managing Editor: Richard Humble
Editor: Christopher Chant
Art Editor: Jim Bridge

CHAPTER 112
Threadbare fortress

Though it is now nearly 30 years after they occurred, there is no difficulty in reconstructing the logical succession of events which in less than 11 months– from June 1944–would take the Western Allies from the Normandy beaches to the heart of the Third Reich. But does this mean that everything was already fore-ordained and that "History", as those who do not know it say, had already rendered its verdict?

Allied landings to be thrown back

On March 20, 1944, Adolf Hitler delivered an appreciation of the situation to the commander-in-chief of his land, sea, and air forces in the Western theatre of operations. By and large, he was less pessimistic with regard to the immediate future than most of his generals, and the arguments he advanced were not without relevance. As he considered the threat assembling on the other side of the Channel, he no doubt remembered his own hesitation in autumn 1940 and the arguments he had put to Mussolini and Count Ciano in January 1941 to excuse his procrastination over Operation *"Seelöwe":*

"We are," he had told them, "in the position of a man with only one cartridge in his rifle. If he misses the target, the situation becomes critical. If the landing fails, we cannot begin again because we would have lost too much *matériel* and the enemy could bring the bulk of his forces into whichever zone he wanted

△ Dusk watch on the Channel at a German flak post. Beach obstacles can be seen on the foreshore.

But so long as the attack has not come, he must always take into account that it may."

And so, according to Rommel, he declared to his generals, whom he summoned that day to the Berghof:

"It is evident that an Anglo-American landing in the West will and must come. How and where it will come no one knows. Equally, no kind of speculation on the subject is possible ... The enemy's entire landing operation must under no circumstances be allowed to last longer than a matter of hours or, at the most, days, with the Dieppe attempt as a model. Once the landing has been defeated it will under no circumstances be repeated by the enemy. Quite apart from the heavy casualties he would suffer, months would be needed to prepare for a renewed attempt. Nor is this the only factor which would deter the Anglo-Americans from trying again. There would also be the crushing blow to their morale which

▽ *and* ▽ ▽ *How the Atlantic Wall defences were portrayed in the German illustrated press: massive cliffs of concrete and guns frowning from their emplacements. But apart from the Pas-de-Calais and a few other sectors the Atlantic Wall had not even been started by the end of 1943.*

a miscarried invasion would inflict. It would, for one thing, prevent the re-election of Roosevelt in America and with luck he would finish up somewhere in jail. In England, too, war-weariness would assert itself even more greatly than hitherto and Churchill, in view of his age and his illness, and with his influence now on the wane, would no longer be in a position to carry through a new landing operation. We could counter the numerical strength of the enemy – about 50 to 60 divisions – within a very short time, by forces of equal strength. The destruction of the enemy's landing attempt means more than a purely local decision on the Western front. It is the sole decisive factor in the whole conduct of the war and hence in its final result."

And so Hitler made the final issue of the conflict depend on the check that his enemies would receive during the first hours of the landing on the coasts of France. Hitler's vision was clear. There can be no doubt that a defeat of the nature of the one suffered by the 2nd Canadian Division at Dieppe, but five

△ △ *A stepped concrete gun embrasure, designed to give maximum shelter from offshore bombardment and air bombing.*
△ *Anti-tank wall. Both sides learned from the Dieppe raid, where the sea wall had thwarted the attempt to push Churchill tanks off the beaches.*

times as great, would have struck a terrible blow at the morale of the British and Americans. Nor can there be any doubt that long months, perhaps even a year, would have passed before the Allies could launch another attack.

By that time, O.K.H. would have received the necessary means from the West to stabilise the situation between the Black Sea and the Gulf of Finland, while the Luftwaffe and the Kriegsmarine would have once more challenged the British and Americans by bringing new arms of terrifying efficiency into use.

New weapons

---

1. V-1 and V-2

It is, in fact, well known that the strides forward taken by German science in the field of jet propulsion could have taken a heavy toll of the British and American bomber squadrons if they had been applied with priority to fighter interception. In addition to (and in spite of) the delays caused by the bombing of Peenemünde on the night of the August 17–18, 1943, the Luftwaffe was ready to undertake once more its attack on London with the help of its V-1 flying bomb and V-2 rocket. The former, flying at a maximum speed of 410 mph, was still within the capacity of fighter defence and anti-aircraft fire, but not so the V-2. This was a real missile in the sense in which we now use the word. It plunged on to its target at a speed close to 2,350 mph and was unstoppable. These missiles, carrying nearly a ton of explosive, had a range of between 190 and 250 miles. Moreover, these terrible weapons were highly economical, both in money and labour.

2. The 'Schnorkel'

At the time when Hitler was expressing the opinions just quoted, U-boats fitted with the *Schnorkel* (or more properly *Schnorchel*) device were first appearing in the Atlantic. This device had been invented in the Netherlands, and consisted of a retractable pipe through which, so long as it stayed at a depth of 20 to 25 feet under water, a U-boat could run its diesels and vent its exhaust. The U-boats could also recharge their batteries without surfacing and remain under water for weeks on end.

It has been calculated that from summer 1944 the *Schnorkel* had become so common that the success rate of Allied

◁ ◁ *"Dragon's Teeth" tank obstacles—concrete pyramids festooned with barbed wire to discourage infantry infiltration as well—shield a sector on the Dutch coast.*

△ *Too late for Dönitz. One of the superb new Type XXI U-boats with which Hitler, clutching at any straw, boasted that he would win the Battle of the Atlantic in 1944, lies impotently in dry dock with one of its smashed predecessors slumped against its flank.*

◁ *Genuine advantage for the U-boat arm: a boat fitted with an air-breathing Schnorkel.*

▷ *The offensive rôle of the Atlantic Wall: huge, concrete-armoured U-boat pens under construction.*
▷ ▷ *Genesis of the modern inter-continental ballistic missile: V-1 and V-2, Hitler's "doodle-bug" and rocket bomb, with which he swore to raze London from bases in western Europe. Capturing these missile sites would be an important task for the Allied forces.*

destroyers in their battle against the submarines had fallen by half. But there is a bad side to everything and, some 15 years ago, Admiral Barjot wrote in this connection:

"On the other hand, the *Schnorkel* slowed down their strategic speed. From a surface speed of 17 knots (20 mph) the *Schnorkel*–equipped submarines found their rate reduced to six knots (6 or 7 mph). The unavoidable delays in reaching their targets were doubled or even tripled."

The consequences he drew can be illustrated by the following: of the 120 operational boats, 39 were in port and 81 at sea. Of the last, 64 were in transit and only 17 actually in their operational sectors.

"So," Barjot concludes, "in April 1942, though the number of operational submarines was similar, only 23 per cent of them were in transit, whereas after the *Schnorkel* had been fitted, half of the U-boats were in transit."

Therefore at best the *Schnorkel* was only a palliative for the problems faced by Dönitz, and there was even another disadvantage: it appeared on the screens of the new British and American radar

The German Fieseler FZG-76 (V-1) flying bomb

Engine: one Argus As 014 pulse jet, 740 lb static thrust.
Warhead: 1,870 lb of high explosive.
Speed: 410 mph.
Range: 150 miles.
Ceiling: 9,150 feet.
Cruise: 360 mph at 2,500 feet.
Weight loaded: 4,858 lbs.
Span: 17 feet $8\frac{1}{4}$ inches.
Length: 25 feet $4\frac{3}{4}$ inches.
(V stands for *Vergeltungswaffe* or Revenge Weapon).

The German Peenemünde A-4 (V-2) ballistic missile

Engine: one liquid oxygen- and ethyl alcohol-fuelled liquid propellant rocket, 70,000 lbs of thrust.
Warhead: 2,150 lbs of high explosive.
Speed: 3,440 miles per hour maximum.
Range: 185 miles.
Weight loaded: 28,500 lbs.
Diameter: 5 feet 5 inches.
Height: 46 feet 11 inches.
Span: 11 feet 8 inches (across fins).

sets operating on centrimetric wave-lengths.

3. The Type XXI . . .

On the other hand, if the Type XXI and XXVI U-boats had come into service earlier, they might have been able to change the course of the submarine war.

The Type XXI U-boat, beautifully designed, was driven under water by two electric engines with a total of 500 horsepower. These enabled it to travel for an hour and a half at the up till then unheard of speed of 18 knots (21 mph) or for ten hours at a speed of between 12 and 14 knots (14 or 16 mph). It could, therefore, hunt convoys while submerged and then easily avoid the attack of the convoy escort. Furthermore, it was remarkably silent and could dive to a depth of more than 675 feet, an advantage not to be scorned in view of the limitations of the listening devices used by its enemies.

Dönitz intended to use prefabricated

◁ ◁ Above and below: *V-1s are prepared for launching, and one is shown taking off. About the size of a fighter aircraft the V-1 was powered by a pulse-jet which emitted a characteristic guttural drone, hence its other nickname "buzz-bomb". The pulse-jet cut out over the target and the missile plunged to earth. That was the theory; they were wildly erratic machines.*

◁ *Engineers prepare a V-2 rocket for launching. The V-2 was a much more formidable proposition than the V-1 as its approach could not be detected.*

△ *and* ▽ *How they looked in flight – the sinister dagger-shape of the V-1 with its stabbing pulse-jet exhaust flame, and the streamlined shape of a V-2 lifting off.*

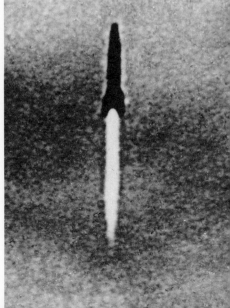

▽ *Fire-control centre in one of the big German coastal batteries.*

▷ ▷ Above and below: *The man who nearly made a myth into a terrifying reality for the Allies: Erwin Rommel. Within weeks of being appointed to inspect the defences of the West he had toured the entire coast from the Pyrenees to the Danish frontier and was horrified with how little he found. Rommel threw himself into his new task with characteristic energy. As in Africa in the old days he was everywhere, inspecting, exhorting, criticising, and urging the work forward with every waking minute.*

methods of production and thus hoped to see the new U-boats come off the slipways at a rate of 33 per month from autumn 1944 onwards. The parts would be assembled in three yards, in concrete shelters. But he had failed to take into account the destruction of the German railway system under the hammer blows of British and American strategic bombing, and so the pieces which had been prefabricated in the heart of the country reached the assembly shops at very irregular intervals.

And, in fact, of this class of ship, only *U-2511* (Lieutenant-Commander A. Schnee) actually went to sea on service. This was on April 30, 1945.

4. . . . and XXVI U-boats

The Type XXVI U-boat was driven, both on the surface and underwater, by a Walter turbine which used hydrogen peroxide and could reach, even while submerged, speeds of 24 knots (28 mph), that is four times the best performance claimed for its British or American rivals.

But neither type was operational by the time Germany capitulated. The fact is, however, that after the war, the Type XXVI U-boat was copied by all the navies of the world, and has sailed in particular under the Soviet flag, which calls to mind, inevitably, that imitation is the sincerest form of flattery.

Evidently then, the Führer had quite a number of good cards up his sleeve, but only—as he himself admitted—provided that his Western enemies could be wiped out on the beaches on the very day they landed, for the Wehrmacht could no longer fight a long holding battle between the rivers Orne and Vire. The situation demanded unquestionably that victory in the West should be swift, so that the victors could be sent with the minimum delay to the Eastern Front.

But the least that can be said is that on this front, considered decisive by Hitler, the German high command was as badly organised as it could possibly be, perhaps by virtue of the principle "divide and rule".

On the other side of the English Channel, General Eisenhower had absolute control not only over the land forces in his theatre of operations, but also over the naval forces under Admiral Sir Bertram Ramsey and over the Tactical Air Forces commanded by Air Chief-Marshal Sir Trafford Leigh-Mallory. He also retained overall command of Lieutenant-General Carl A. Spaatz's Strategic Air Force. The situation was quite different at Saint-Germain-en-Laye, headquarters of the Commander-in-Chief West or O.B.W. *(Oberbefehlshaber West)* and at la Roche-Guyon, headquarters of Army Group "B".

Lack of co-operation

In short, Field-Marshal von Rundstedt was not entitled to give orders to Admiral Krancke, who commanded German naval forces in the West, to Field-Marshal Sperrle, head of *Luftflotte* III, to General Pickert, who commanded III Anti-Aircraft Corps. Krancke came directly under the command of Grand-Admiral Dönitz, and the two others were responsible to *Reichs-*

marschall Göring. Of course Krancke had only a small number of light ships and Sperrle found his forces reduced by June 6, 1944 to 419 aircraft, 172 of which were fighters. Nevertheless, considering that the aim was to destroy the enemy on the beaches, the lack of co-ordination between the three arms was to have catastrophic consequences for Germany.

In regard to the Navy it should be said that though Rommel, commanding Army Group "B", had a judiciously chosen naval attaché on his staff in the person of Vice-Admiral Ruge, he still could not manage to make Krancke lay down a sufficiently thick minefield in the estuary of the Seine. Yet the Germans possessed a mine triggered by the pressure wave of a ship passing over it, and this could have

CIMETIÈRE DES ALLIÉS

△ *Rommel, complete with his familiar desert goggles, holds a snap conference on Panzer tactics in the field. Thanks to Hitler's vacillation he failed to get complete control of all Panzer units in France, which was to have serious effects on the German defensive deployment.*
▷ *Intended to prevent French hopes from getting too high: the spectre of Dieppe is evoked by German propaganda.*

proved a devastating weapon.

In addition to these already considerable failings, naval gunners and army men could not reach agreement on the question of coastal batteries, their location, and the fire control methods to be used. The ex-Commander-in-Chief in Norway, Colonel-General von Falkenhorst, later expressed his thoughts in terms which were rather critical of his naval colleagues, when he wrote:

"When I look back, I can see that responsibilities were badly apportioned, and that this brought several mistakes in its train. The results were severe overwork, difficulties, and conflict. Army artillery officers had received a totally different training from the naval gunners, a training which had developed under very different sets of circumstances. Moreover, the ideas of the older senior officers–the generals and the admirals–on the problems often differed greatly. The locations of covered or uncovered batteries, camouflage, the setting of obstacles, etc, were in general fields which were entirely new to the naval gunners, since these problems never arose on board their ships, and, consequently, did not appear in their training schedules. They used naval guns as they had been installed by the engineers and could not or would not change anything at all. The result of this was that, all along the coast, batteries were set in the open, near the beaches, so that they were at the mercy of the direct fire of every enemy landing ship but could not effectively contribute to the defence of the coast. There followed several most unhappy conflicts between generals and admirals."

Falkenhorst, who had installed 34 coastal defence batteries covering the approaches to Bergen, would seem competent to level these criticisms. Some of these guns, between Narvik and Harstad, were of 16-inch calibre. It is nonetheless true that the naval gunners also had some right on their side, because the army gunners thought they could hit moving targets like ships by using indirect fire methods.

Göring's malign influence

The deployment of anti-aircraft forces also created new tension between the arms. This time the disagreement arose between the commanders of the land and air forces, under whose joint command the anti-aircraft defences came. Rommel knew, better than anyone else, how efficient the 8.8-cm anti-aircraft gun could be when used as an anti-tank gun, and he would have liked to place a large number of such batteries between the Orne and the Vire. But Göring was obstinately opposed to any such redeployment and Rommel had to resign himself to not having his own way.

This tension lasted after the Allied landing, and brought these bitter words from Colonel-General Sepp Dietrich of the *Waffen*-S.S., commander of the 5th *Panzerarmee*:

"I constantly ordered these guns to stay forward and act in an anti-tank rôle against Allied armour. My orders were just as often countermanded by Pickert, who moved them back into the rear areas to protect administrative sites. I asked time and time again that these guns be put under my command, but I was always told by the High Command that it was

impossible."

On the other hand, Major-General Plocher, chief-of-staff of *Luftflotte* III at the time, has taken up the cudgels for Pickert:

"We had insisted on these guns being controlled by Luftwaffe officers because the army did not know how to handle such equipment. There was always a great deal of argument about who was to deploy the 88's but Field-Marshal von Rundstedt finally allowed us to chose our own localities." He adds, with a sting in the tail: "This was necessary in order to prevent the army from squandering both men and equipment. We used to say that the German infantryman would always fight until the last anti-aircraft man."

The least that can be said of these incoherent remarks is that, though Rommel and Rundstedt had received orders to wipe out the Allied landings in the shortest time possible, they were refused part of the means necessary to carry out their orders.

△ *The work goes forward. More concrete defences are piled up at Lorient. The Atlantic ports were the natural foci for the extension of the Atlantic Wall complex.*

Mined stakes   "Belgian gates"   Gun emplacements

Log obstacles   "Czech hedgehogs"   Above water
                                       Below water

"Tetrahydra"   Machine gun positions

Low tide   Mid tide   High tide   Minefields

ATLANTIC WALL: THE ROMMEL PLAN

How Rommel planned to win the "battle of the beaches"—with a sketch he made to show how the various elements of the foreshore defences should be integrated. Whatever the state of the tide when the Allies finally landed, he hoped to keep their assault troops floundering on the beaches under constant fire until they lost heart and re-embarked. This diagram shows all the main obstacles planted along the invasion beaches, in the form they would have taken if Rommel had been given a few more months to extend and complete the defences.

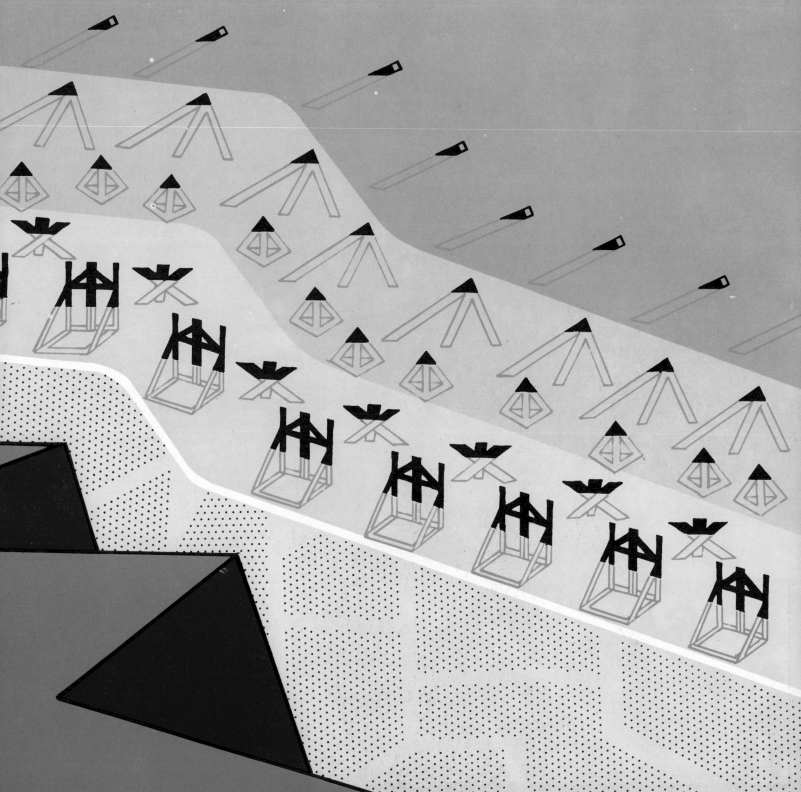

CHAPTER 113

Rommel's achievement

△ *Rommel (left) confers on the siting of a new battery with German Navy officers. His chief Navy liaison man, Admiral Ruge, found that Rommel's no-nonsense approach made him an easy man to work with over practicalities.*

▽ *German flak crew goes through gun-drill . . .*
▷ *. . . as do their comrades on a torpedo-boat.*

On D-Day, Rundstedt, as Commander-in-Chief in the West, had the following under his command: two army groups ("B" and "G"), comprising four armies (7th, 15th, 1st, and 19th). These in turn had 15 corps between them, totalling 40 infantry, four parachute, four Luftwaffe field, nine Panzer, and one *Panzergrenadier* divisions.

However, for all this it is by no means true that Rundstedt exercised over this force the authority normally given to a commander-in-chief. In the first place, the Luftwaffe units (one corps, eight divisions) were only under his tactical command; the same was true of his four *Waffen*-S.S. divisions and the I S.S. Panzer Corps. He had no authority over these units in the questions of training, promotions, the appointment of commanders or in the field of discipline. That is what Hitler cruelly reminded Rommel, who had requested that action be taken against the 2nd *"Das Reich"* Panzer Division of the *Waffen*-S.S., after the appalling massacre at Oradour-sur-Glâne.

Even more, O.B.W. had had it made quite clear that it could not, without the Führer's permission, move two of its best armoured divisions, the 12th *"Hitlerjugend"* *Waffen*-S.S. Panzer Division, stationed near Lisieux, and the 130th Panzer-*"Lehr"* Division, formed the previous winter from Panzer instructors and now stationed around Châteaudun. Moreover, O.K.W. did not cease interfering in Rundstedt's sphere of command, as the latter explained bitterly to the British officers who questioned him after his capture:

"I did not have my way. As Commander-in-Chief in the West my only authority was to change the guards in front of my gate."

As will be seen later, everything confirms the truth of this account. Therefore it appears that Hitler did not appreciate the complete incompatibility between despotic, arrogant, and meddling authority, and the need to make rapid decisions, the vital importance of which he soon came to recognise.

Where would the Allies land?

A major part of the success of the landings can be explained by the inefficiency of the German Intelligence services. Here the Nazis Kaltenbrunner and Schellenberg, who had ousted the professionals Canaris and Oster, could neither get a clear idea of the British and American plans nor escape being deceived by the Allies' diversionary manoeuvres. Therefore hypotheses were the order of the day

at O.K.W. as well as Saint-Germain-en-Laye, headquarters of Western Command (O.B.W.) and la Roche-Guyon, headquarters of Army Group "B".

Hitler had given a long analysis on the situation on March 20. Though he recognised that there was no way of being sure in which area the Allies would land, over the whole coastline from Norway to Greece, he nevertheless made his point:

"At no place along our long front is a landing impossible, except perhaps where the coast is broken by cliffs. The most

suitable and hence the most threatened areas are the two west coast peninsulas, Cherbourg and Brest, which are very tempting and offer the best possibilities for the formation of a bridgehead, which would then be enlarged systematically by the use of air forces and heavy weapons of all kinds."

This hypothesis was perfectly logical and the order of battle of the German 7th Army (Colonel-General Dollmann), was correctly arranged to face this possibility. Of its 14 divisions, 12 were deployed between the Rivers Vire and Loire.

Rundstedt did not share Hitler's opinion, and considered that there were a great many more advantages from the Allied point of view for them to cross the Channel and land in the Pas-de-Calais. Later, in 1945, he supported his views by using these arguments, according to Milton Shulman:

"In the first place an attack from Dover against Calais would be using the shortest sea route to the Continent. Secondly, the V-1 and V-2 sites were located in this area. Thirdly this was the shortest route to the Ruhr and the heart of industrial Germany, and once a successful landing had been made it would take only four days to reach the Rhine. Fourthly, such an operation would sever the forces in Northern France from those along the Mediterranean coast. Against the Pas-de-Calais being chosen was the fact that this area had the strongest coastal defences, and was the only part of the Atlantic Wall that even remotely lived up to its reputation. I always used to tell my staff that if I was Montgomery I would attack the Pas-de-Calais."

But this would have meant coming up against the strongest part of the Atlantic Wall, whose concrete-housed batteries on either side of Cape Gris-Nez kept the English coast between Ramsgate and

◁ ◁ *Two German reservists, recalled to the colours, relax in the trenches.*
◁▽ *Wheeling a "Belgian Gate" into position on the foreshore— a massive construction of angle-iron designed to disembowel landing-craft. There were other unpleasant surprises, too—but never enough of them to satisfy Rommel.*
▽ *Like an outsize concrete bolster—a tank trap doubling as a parapet for the infantry behind.*

Dungeness under the fire of their 14 11-, 12-, 15-, and 16-inch guns; also Colonel-General von Salmuth's 15th Army was well deployed in the area, with 18 divisions between Antwerp and Cabourg. These troops were of good quality, and so it would seem that at O.K.W. Field-Marshal Keitel and Generals Jodl and Warlimont expected a landing between the mouths of the Rivers Somme and Seine, outside the range of the heavy artillery mentioned above but still within the 15th Army's sector.

Rommel's anxieties

Rommel commanded Army Group "B", which included the 7th and 15th Armies and LXXXVIII Corps, with three divisions for the defence of Holland. His main worry was the weakness of the defences on the beaches of the bay of the Seine, where three divisions were thinly stretched between Cabourg (exclusive) and the port of Cherbourg. More important, this weakness was not compensated for by the density or heavy calibre of the coastal artillery. Actually, on the 125-mile front between Le Havre and Cape Barfleur, the Swedish coastal artillery expert Colonel Stjernfelt has identified only 18 batteries, 12 of which could not reach the Calvados beaches or did not fire at all on D-Day.

Another concern of Rommel's was what form he should give to this defensive battle for which he was responsible and which might begin any day. But on this question, his point of view was almost exactly the same as the Führer's, detailed above.

In his opinion, a sea-borne landing differs from a ground attack essentially in that the latter has its maximum force on the first day of the offensive. It then decreases in momentum because of the losses that are suffered and logistic difficulties. This allows the defending army to put off its counter-attack. On the other hand, the enemy who comes from the sea will be weak at the moment of landing, but will become steadily stronger within his bridgehead, so that any delay at all in the counter-attack will reduce in like proportion its chance of success.

The Panzers were indubitably the best means of counter-attack, and so the sensible thing was to deploy them in such a manner that they could be hurled against the enemy wherever he might appear (Low Countries, Pas-de-Calais, Normandy, or Brittany) on the actual day of the landing. This is what Rommel explained in a letter to Jodl on April 23, 1944:

"If, in spite of the enemy's air superiority, we succeed in getting a large part of our mobile force into action in the threatened coast defence sectors in the first few hours, I am convinced that the enemy attack on the coast will collapse completely on its first day."

But he added: "My only real anxiety

concerns the mobile forces. Contrary to what was decided at the conference on the 21st March, they have so far not been placed under my command. Some of them are dispersed over a large area inland, which means they will arrive too late to play any part in the battle for the coast. With the heavy enemy air superiority we can expect, any large-scale movement of motorised forces to the coast will be exposed to air attacks of tremendous weight and long duration. But without rapid assistance from the armoured divisions and mobile units, our coast divisions will be hard put to it to counter attacks coming simultaneously from the sea and from airborne troops inland. Their land front is too thinly held for that. The dispositions of both combat and reserve forces should be such as to ensure that the minimum possible movement will be required to counter an attack at any of most likely points . . . and to ensure that the greater part of the enemy troops, sea and airborne, will be destroyed by our fire during their approach."

This led him to conclude: "The most decisive battle of the war, and the fate of

◁ *A foreshore sector, sown with defences in concentric belts, seen at low tide.*
◁◁ *Gun emplacement under camouflage net.*
◁▽ *Stone cairns—another simple landing-craft obstacle.*

△ *Japan's military attaché, General Komatsu, chats with a Todt Organisation official on the Channel coast.*

▽ Simplicissimus *comments on Churchill and Roosevelt hesitating before taking the plunge in the "bath of blood". Overleaf: The impregnability of the Atlantic Wall, as portrayed by Germany's magazine* Signal.

△ △ *Dollmann, commander of 7th Army in Normandy.*
△ *von Geyr, commander of Panzergruppe "West".*
▽ *Bayerlein, commander of the Panzer-"Lehr" Division.*
▷ *Wehrmacht deployment in the West.*

the German people itself, is at stake. Failing a tight command in one single hand of all the forces available for defence, failing the early engagement of all our mobile forces in the battle for the coast, victory will be in grave doubt. If I am to wait until the enemy landing has actually taken place, before I can demand, through normal channels, the command and dispatch of the mobile forces, delays will be inevitable. This will mean that they will probably arrive too late to intervene successfully in the battle for the coast and prevent the enemy landing. A second Nettuno, a highly undesirable situation for us, could result . . ."

And, in fact, after the conference of March 20, Rommel had received from the Führer the right to have *Panzergruppe* "West" put immediately under his direct command. This force, under General Geyr von Schweppenburg, constituted Rundstedt's armoured reserve and, on D-Day, consisted of:

1. I *Waffen* S.S. Panzer Corps;
2. 1st *"Leibstandarte Adolf Hitler"* S.S. Panzer Division (at Beverloo, 45 miles east of Antwerp);
3. 2nd Panzer Division (at Amiens);
4. 116th Panzer Division (in the Gisors–Beauvais region);
5. 12th *"Hitlerjugend"* S.S. Panzer Division (in the Evreux–Lisieux region);
6. 130th Panzer-*"Lehr"* Division (near Châteaudun); and
7. 21st Panzer Division (at Saint-Pierre-sur-Dives, 20 miles south-east of Caen).

But no order had come from O.K.W. to give executive force to Hitler's concession. And so Schweppenburg refused the rôle which Rommel allotted to him. His view was that the Western Front's armoured reserve should be concentrated in a central position downstream from Paris, so that it could intervene with all its strength in that sector where it looked as if the enemy was about to make his main push, after all tricks and feinting movements had been discounted. From this point of view, the way that Army Group "B" at la Roche-Guyon wanted to distribute the Panzers seemed to fit the verdict that Frederick the Great had proclaimed against all systems of wide-stretched defence: *"Wer alles defendieren will, defendiert gar nichts"* (He who tries to defend everything, defends nothing).

Rundstedt, and also Colonel-General Guderian, agreed with this point of view, which could clearly be defended on the principles of war. But were they applicable in those circumstances? Rommel denied that they were and cited as an example, as has been seen, his North African experience. His opponents had not had this experience as they had all come from the Eastern Front, where the enemy's tactical air force was only just beginning to show its power to paralyse ground movement. Events showed that his reasoning was without doubt the more pertinent. However that may be and in spite of his attempt on April 23, Rommel received no satisfaction on this vital point. Better—or worse still—depending on one's point of view, the Führer was equally negative when Rommel suggested that he should advance the Panzer-*"Lehr"* Division to between the Orne and the Vire, deploy the *"Hitlerjugend"* Division in the region of Saint-Lô, and reinforce this sector, which seemed dangerously weak to Rommel, by a brigade of *Nebelwerfers* (976 15-, 21-, and 30-cm barrels) and a large number of heavy (8.8-cm) anti-aircraft batteries. Faced with silence from Hitler, Rommel left la Roche-Guyon at dawn on June 4 for Berchtesgaden, not without having consulted his barometer and obtained Rundstedt's leave.

Hitler's personality ensures failure

In spite of the documents published since 1945, Hitler's attitude when faced with the problems of the German high command remains incomprehensible, for it abounds in contradictions. The facts speak for themselves.

Though he did not believe the forecasts of his subordinates at O.K.W. and of Rundstedt, all of whom envisaged the British and the Americans approaching the French coast between Le Havre and the Pas-de-Calais, he accepted their forecast the day after the Allies landed in the bay of the Seine and stuck to it obstinately until a decisive hole was punched in the German line on the left bank of the Vire by the 1st American Army. In fact he was convinced, up to July 24, that the only purpose of the Battle of Normandy was to trick him into lowering his guard in the Pas-de-Calais.

Furthermore, though his hypothesis of March 20, concerning the first objec-

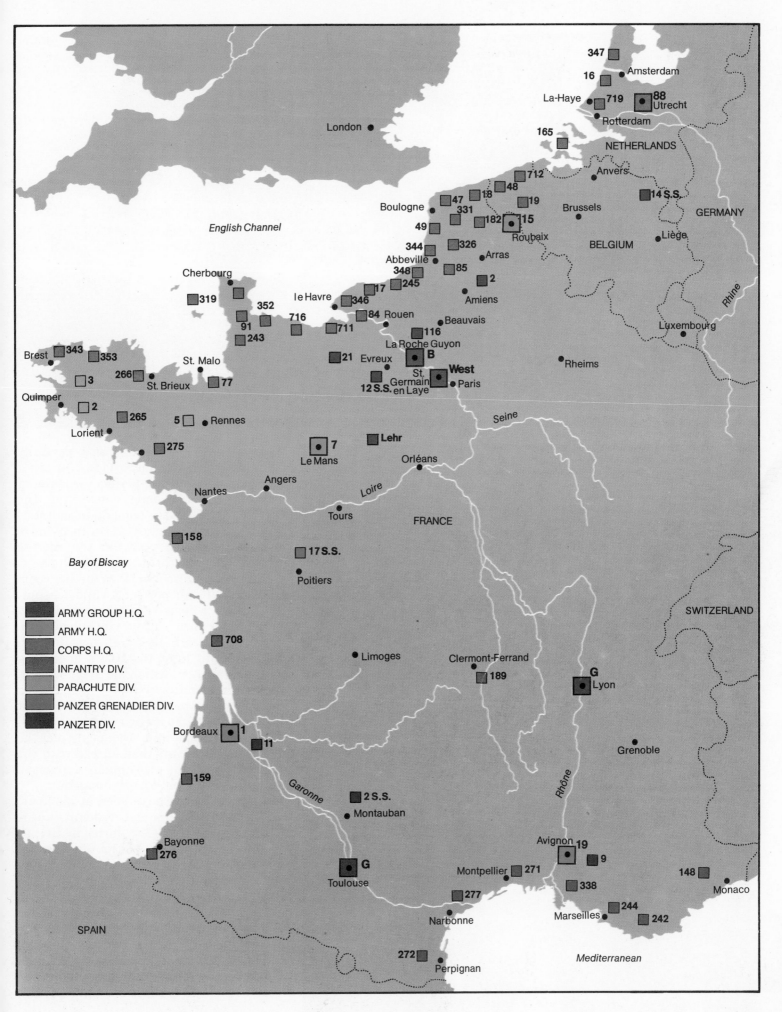

ARMY GROUP H.Q.
ARMY H.Q.
CORPS H.Q.
INFANTRY DIV.
PARACHUTE DIV.
PANZER GRENADIER DIV.
PANZER DIV.

English Channel

London

Amsterdam
La-Haye
Rotterdam
Utrecht
NETHERLANDS
Anvers
Brussels
BELGIUM
Liège
GERMANY
Luxembourg
Rhine

347
16
719
88
165
712
14 S.S.
48
18
47
331
19
49
182
115
Roubaix
344
326
Arras
Abbeville
348
85
2
245
Amiens
17
346
Beauvais
84 Rouen
716
711
116
243
La Roche Guyon
91
21 Evreux
B
352
West
St. Germain en Laye
Paris
319
12 S.S.
Cherbourg
le Havre

Brest
343
353
St. Malo
266
3
77
St. Brieux
Quimper
2
265
5 Rennes
Lorient
275
Lehr
7
Le Mans
Orléans
Angers
Nantes
Loire
Tours
FRANCE
Seine

Bay of Biscay

158

17 S.S.
Poitiers

708
Limoges
Clermont-Ferrand
189
G
Lyon
SWITZERLAND
Grenoble

Bordeaux
1
11
159
Garonne
2 S.S.
Montauban
Rhône
Avignon
19
9
Bayonne
276
G
Toulouse
Montpellier
271
148
Monaco
277
338
244
Narbonne
Marseilles
242
SPAIN
272
Perpignan
Mediterranean

1565

tives of the Allied attack, only partially coincided with Rommel's views, in other respects there was perfect agreement between the two men concerning the way to repel it: an immediate counter-attack on the beaches so as to avoid a long battle of attrition, like the one the armies had fought at Anzio–Nettuno.

But here there came a further contradiction. If, for perfectly valid reasons, the Führer rejected the plans of deployment put forward by Geyr von Schweppenburg, he nevertheless refused Rommel the means to fight the battle according to the plans on which he had been in entire agreement with him. Though it is a risky business to try to rewrite history, it will be noted that if Hitler had drawn all the conclusions from the principles he had enunciated, and had agreed with the suggestions of his distinguished general, the following would have happened:

1. Rommel would have been at his head-quarters at la Roche-Guyon on June 6, and would have been alerted by British and American parachute drops, slightly after 0130 hours, while in the event he only knew of them five hours later while still at his private house in Herrlingen on the outskirts of Ulm.

2. The counter-attack launched in the afternoon of June 6 by just the 21st Panzer Division in only the British sector, could have been executed by the Panzer-"*Lehr*" Division and the 12th

Four views of Rommel, taken during the last months before D-Day. Behind the furious energy with which he urged on the laying of minefields and the construction of energy lay a carefully worked-out strategy, born of the painful lessons learned in Africa. These were the effectiveness of the minefield and the paramount need to deny the enemy freedom to manoeuvre—or to establish a foothold and make it too strong to eliminate. Rommel forecast—with complete accuracy—that the battle for Normandy would really be won on the beaches.

The men of the Atlantic Wall:
△ Workers pressing on with the uncompleted defences ...
▷ ... the soldier who would have to defend them.

"Hitlerjugend" S.S. Panzer Division. From the positions which Rommel wanted them to occupy, they could have simultaneously attacked the bridgeheads that the Americans were establishing. By reinforcing these two with 400 or 450 tanks and assault guns, the first would almost certainly have wiped out "Omaha" Beach before nightfall and the second was well-placed to attack the poorly placed parachute units around Saint-Mère-Eglise.

True enough, if this had in fact happened, the Panzer-"Lehr" would have found itself under the fire of the Allied naval forces, and the precedents of Gela and Salerno showed how redoubtable and efficient their heavy shells were against tanks. This argument had been used by Geyr von Schweppenburg during the stormy arguments he had had with Rommel about the distribution of armoured divisions. But though this was a real danger, does it follow that they should have abstained from any attack at all on D-Day and that they should not have taken advantage of the fleeting moment when the enemy had not yet consolidated his bridgeheads?

CHAPTER 114
Allied air offensive

Britain's best heavy bomber of
World War II: an Avro
Lancaster B. I of No. 50
Squadron in flight.

By 1943 ruins were piling up from one end of the Third Reich to the other, the effect of night raids by R.A.F. Bomber Command and day raids by the American 8th Air Force, joined by the 15th Air Force from October 9 from their air base at Foggia, hastily brought back into action after its capture by the British 8th Army on September 27. These round-the-clock attacks were the result of a plan adopted at Casablanca late in January 1943 at a meeting of the British and American Combined Chiefs-of-Staff Committee. The various objectives were given the following priorities:

"(a) German submarine construction yards.
(b) The German aircraft industry.
(c) Transportation.
(d) Oil plants.
(e) Other targets in enemy war industry."

This order was several times revised. After they had dropped 63 per cent of their bombs on submarine construction yards at Emden, Wilhelmshaven, Bremen, Hamburg, Flensburg, Kiel, and Lübeck and against their reinforced concrete pens at Brest, Lorient, St. Nazaire, and Bordeaux in what turned out to be perfectly useless attacks, the Americans put this objective at the bottom of their list. So did the British after they had expended 30 per cent of their bombs. Also, by the end of 1943 the U-boat menace was no longer pressing. It should be recalled that in order to keep up his U-boat campaign against all opposition Dönitz was at this time claiming that to abandon it would subject Germany's cities to even greater ordeals as enemy bombing raids grew in ferocity. In this he was not mistaken.

Difficulties in co-ordination

It had not been easy for the British and the Americans to come to an agreement over the best use of the U.S. 8th Air Force. The first unit of this force had arrived in Great Britain on July 1, 1942 when the Flying Fortress "Jarring Jenny" had touched down at Prestwick airport in Scotland and an 8th Air Force materials control officer had entered into his log-book: "Entry flying equipment: one B-17E; total: 1."

It was the opinion of Air Chief-Marshal Sir Charles Portal, Chief of the Air Staff, that the squadrons of Flying Fortresses

◁ *Smoke billows up from the Bettenhausen factory in Kassel (outlined in white) as one of the attacking B-17 bombers of the U.S. 8th Air Force passes over the target area.*
◁▽ *The crew of the Flying Fortress "Blue Dreams" in cheerful mood after completing a mission.*
△ *General Carl A. Spaatz, head of the 8th Air Force in 1942 and of the U.S. Strategic Air Forces, comprising the 8th and 15th Air Forces, from January 1944.*
▽ *A damaged Flying Fortress under repair at a Mobile Machine Shop.*

The American Boeing B-17G Flying Fortress heavy bomber

Engines: four Wright R-1820 Cyclone radials, 1,200-hp each.
Armament: thirteen .5-inch Browning machine guns and up to 17,600 lbs of bombs.
Speed: 300 mph at 30,000 feet.
Ceiling: 35,000 feet.
Range: 1,850 miles with typical bomb-load.
Weight empty/loaded: 32,720/55,000 lbs.
Span: 103 feet 9½ inches.
Length: 74 feet 4 inches.
Height: 19 feet 1 inch.
Crew: 10.

should take part in the night bombing raids of Bomber Command, whose C.-in-C. naturally welcomed the idea of having eventually twice or three times as many planes at his disposal. Both men thought that day bombing against A.A. and Göring's fighters would suffer unbearable losses for a very mediocre profit. At the Pentagon, General H. H. Arnold, U.S.A.A.F. Chief-of-Staff, and at H.Q. 8th Air Force, Lieutenant-General Ira C. Eaker both disagreed with British optimism about night operations. If the Anglo-American strategic force was to carry out its mission successfully it would, in their opinion, have to attack by day and nothing would make them change their minds. But if, under certain conditions,

△ *Ammunitioning the ball turret, aptly named "The Morgue", of a B-17 with .5-inch armour piercing tracer rounds. Once ensconced in the cramped turret, sitting on a bicycle seat and braced against padded knee-rests, the ball gunner was condemned to spend the whole flight there, with little chance of escape in the event of his aircraft being shot down.*

◁ *G. C. Wilson, of Minneapolis, Minnesota, in the rear turret of his Fortress. The swastikas show that he was credited with shooting down of two German fighters. American rear turrets were usually armed with two .5-inch guns, compared with the British practice of four .303-inch weapons.*
▽ *An 8th Air Force Liberator is christened.*

△ Flying Fortress of the 533rd Bombardment Squadron, 381st Bombardment Group, 1st Combat Wing, 1st Air Division, 8th Air Force, over England.

◁ Armourers bomb up a drab-camouflaged B-17F. Note the provision of mounts for machine guns in the plexiglass nose, much improved upon by the fitting of a two-gun chin turret in late production F and all G models.

which were not all fulfilled late in 1942, the Flying Fortresses and the Liberators were to take on the considerable risks of day bombing, this was not to be so for the R.A.F., whatever the courage or the state of training of its crews.

R.A.F. by night, U.S.A.A.F. by day

And so that task was divided round the clock equally between the British and the Americans, the former taking off at nightfall and the latter by day, each sticking to his task with ruthless obstinacy and without complaining of his

losses. This was the system adopted after heated discussions. For Generals Arnold and Eaker there was the additional advantage (though perhaps not admitted) that the Americans would still retain their autonomy though working under a joint command. This division of labour meant that the two air forces came to use totally different methods of action.

By day the 8th Air Force performed what it called precision bombing. Well-defined objectives were thus allotted: a particular factory, construction-yard, assembly-shop in Germany or in an occupied country, in the latter of which only where civilian casualties could be spared as far as was compatible with the successful completion of the mission. The American crews nevertheless greatly exaggerated the degree of precision they could obtain with their Norden bomb-sights.

As it operated by night, Bomber Command could not expect results like these, and so performed area bombing, applying to Germany what nuclear arms specialists today have come to call "anti-city" strategy. In addition to H.E. bombs, they used a great variety of incendiary devices, some packed with jellied products of horrifying efficiency. Air Chief-Marshal Sir Arthur Harris, A.O.C. Bomber Command, did not limit his task to the simple destruction of the Third Reich's war potential, but aimed also at destroying the morale of the German people. In

△ *Captain Donald S. Gentile seated on the wing of his North American P-51 Mustang "Shangri-La". He was one of the 8th Air Force's highest scoring aces, with 20 "kills". Until the advent of the Mustang, with long range tanks, American daylight bomber formations were appallingly vulnerable to the German fighter defences.*

in spite of the loss during the year of 1,261 four-engined planes and most of their crews, the growing strength of the 8th Air Force is shown in the following table:

| | Groups | |
	B-17 Flying Fortresses	B-24 Liberators
January 1	5	2
April 1	5	2
July 1	11	–
October 1	17	4
December 1	19	7

This shows that the number of four-engined bombers at the disposal of Major-General James H. Doolittle, who succeeded Eaker as 8th Air Force commander at the end of the year, increased over three and a half times in 12 months. The number of sorties made by these planes rose at an even faster, one could say spectacular, rate:

January	279
April	379
July	2,334
October	2,159
December	5,618

Flying Fortresses in action

Compared with the Consolidated B-24 Liberator, the American crews operating over Germany preferred the Boeing B-17 Flying Fortress, of which over 12,000 were finally made by a consortium of the original builders with Douglas and Lockheed-Vega. Weighing 24 tons loaded, this four-engined plane could reach a top speed of 325 mph and had a range of 2,000 miles. The B-17E had eleven .3- and .5-inch machine guns which the Americans believed gave it all-round fire-power. This optimism was proved false by experience. For example, on August 17, 1943 the 8th Air Force lost 60 out of the 376 Flying Fortresses sent on raids on the Schweinfurt ball-bearing factory and the Messerschmitt assembly plant at Regensburg. On October 14 a new attack on the first of these objectives cost another 60 planes out of the 291 which had taken off, and altogether the loss of aircraft on these raids over the month was running at the intolerably high level of 8.4 per cent. Under these conditions it can be imagined that questions were raised as to whether or not the methods advocated by General Arnold were failing for, if it was relatively easy to replace the planes, it was not the

this he was free to act. Returning to the matter after the event, he wrote that the Casablanca Conference released him from his last moral scruples. His hands from that time forward were free as far as the bombing war was concerned.

After this account of the basic methods used by the Anglo-American forces in their air offensive against Germany we must now consider briefly the material means which they used with varying success.

From January 1 to December 31, 1943,

△ △ Bombing up a Handley-Page Hampden, Britain's best bomber, together with the Vickers Wellington, during the first two years of the war. The Hampden could carry a worthwhile load a considerable range, but had a completely inadequate defensive armament. The type was phased out of service with Bomber Command by September 1942, but continued as a minelayer and torpedo bomber with Coastal Command until 1944.
△ In the cockpit of an R.A.F. bomber.
▷ The bomb-aimer's position in the nose of a Short Stirling.
▷ △ Armstrong-Whitworth Whitley, another of Britain's standard bombers early in the war.
▷ ▷ Two Stirling bombers. Britain's first war-time four-engined heavy bomber, the type entered service in 1940. Note the long under-carriage legs, to give the wings the right angle of attack at take-off.
▷ ▽ Avro Manchester (right), the unsuccessful two-engined precursor of the Lancaster. Note the Wellington in the background.

same thing for the crews and, after the second attack on Schweinfurt some loss of morale was noticeable among their ranks. This can be illustrated by one anecdote quoted by Werner Girbig in his *1000 Tage über Deutschland*. There was a manufacturer's advertisement in a magazine which, occupying a complete page, showed an Army Air Force machine gunner, his eye staring fiercely through the back-sight of his .5-inch gun, which he was aiming at a swarm of Focke-Wulf 190's. The caption read: "Who's afraid of the Big Bad Wolf?"

"An 8th Air Force pilot tore the page out, pinned it up on the blackboard in the Orderly Room and stuck on it a long strip of paper on which he wrote in red ink 'WE ARE'. Every officer, including the Station Commander, added his signature. Then the whole lot was sent back, without comment, to the manufacturer."

At this time, however, the new B-17G Flying Fortress was coming into service. This had a new chin turret below the pilot's seat, mounting two .5-inch guns and covering the blind area of which the enemy fighters had learned to take advantage. This new protective measure would very likely have been insufficient by itself, but in late autumn the 8th Air Force got fighter escorts

throughout their daylight raids. Until then the Republic P-47 Thunderbolts did not have the range to accompany them to beyond the Rhine and back. This situation changed when North American P-51 Mustang , fitted with drop tanks, were brought into service in numbers large enough to be useful.

"H_2S", a new type of radar

At the same time also new British radar equipment, the "H_2S", came into service. This transmitted on a wavelength of three centimetres and threw on to the screen an image of the ground underneath the plane rather like a fluorescent map. The American formations were thus able to choose the riskiest of weather conditions which would keep German planes grounded. Thanks to the simultaneous intervention of all these factors, the 8th Air Force's losses fell by more than half: in November they were 3.9 per cent, in December 3.4 per cent.

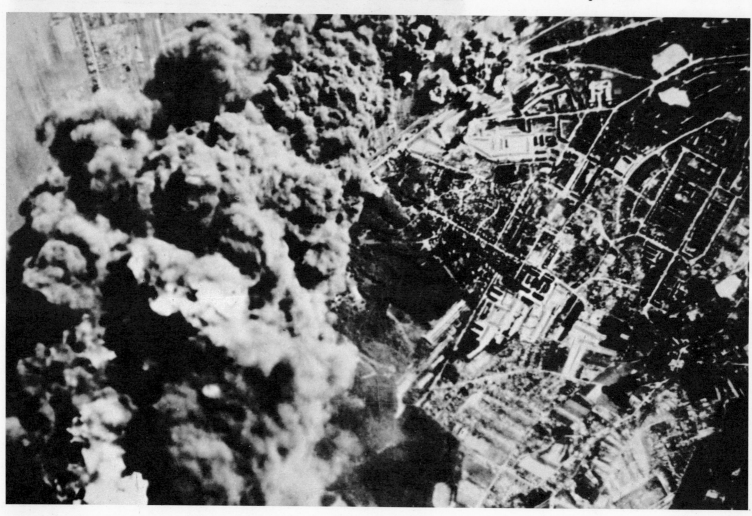

The British four-engined bombers

The R.A.F.'s night offensive was based on three types of four-engined plane:

1. the Avro Lancaster: 28 tons, 287 mph, 1,660 mile range, and eight .303-inch machine guns;
2. the Handley-Page Halifax: 27 tons, 282 mph, 1,030 mile range, and nine .303-inch machine guns; and
3. the Short Stirling: 26.5 tons, 260 mph, 1,930 mile range, and eight .303-inch machine guns.

With the help of Canadian industry 16,000 bombers of these three types were built. Nearly half of them were Lancasters. As will be seen, their armament was insufficient to allow them to carry out daylight raids. They took off at dusk and the device for guiding bombers known as "Gee" then, after March 5, 1943, the "Oboe" blind bombing device, gave them their position at all times and then enabled them to locate their targets with considerable accuracy.

◁ ◁ *Hamburg. The raids between July 24 and August 3, 1943 cost the city some 40,000 dead and informed the Germans of what they could expect in the future.*

◁▽ *Hamburg under the Allied bombardment: in three days 9,000 tons of bombs destroyed 277,000 houses in the city.*

◁ *A low-level photograph taken from a Mosquito during a raid on Hengelo in Holland. Just to the left of the locomotive is a wooden flak tower. Operating at these low altitudes, the speedy Mosquito could drop its bombs with devastating accuracy after passing below the German radar screen on the coast.*

▽ *Reconnaissance photograph of the Focke-Wulf factory at Marienburg in East Prussia, taken on October 9, 1943. The one building not destroyed by direct hits was severely damaged by blast.*

The British Handley-Page Halifax B. II Series la heavy bomber

Engines: four Rolls-Royce Merlin XXII
inlines, 1,460-hp each.
Armament: one .303-inch Vickers "K" gun
and eight .303-inch Browning machine guns
plus 13,000 lbs of bombs.
Speed: 285 mph at 17,500 feet.
Ceiling: 24,000 feet.
Range: 1,860 miles with a 5,800-lb bomb-load.
Weight empty/loaded: 38,250/54,400 lbs.
Span: 98 feet 10 inches.
Length: 70 feet 1 inch.
Height: 20 feet 9 inches.
Crew: 7.

The objective was also indicated by pathfinders using coloured flares. As soon as they came into service they were, of course, fitted with the new "H_2S" radar.

Jamming

It was not enough to see clearly: the enemy also had to be blinded, that is his radar had to be jammed. From late July 1943 the British used a device called "Window". This consisted of thousands and thousands of strips of metallic paper which confused the echoes of the Germans' *Würzburg* apparatus for directing A.A. and fighters. Even better, the British succeeded in breaking in on the enemy radio-traffic between ground control and the fighters up in the air, sending his planes off in the wrong direction by mimicking exactly the ground-controller's voice. In the night of October 22-23, during an attack on Kassel, the authentic German controller, infuriated by the interference, let out an oath and the Luftwaffe pilots heard the "phantom voice" exclaim: "That cretin of an Englishman's starting to swear!" Whereupon the German, beside himself with rage, shouted into the microphone: "It's not the Englishman who's swearing, it's me!"

Germany's cities devastated by bombs

For evident reasons, on their day raids, the Americans rarely sent in more than 200 planes on the same objective. By night the British attacked the towns of the Reich with three and sometimes five times as many and made the raids last as long as possible so as to saturate the active and the passive defence, particularly the latter which, within two hours after the raids had begun, was faced with hundreds of fires concealing delayed-action bombs. Sometimes in these two hours 1,500 and even 2,000 tons of bombs were dropped.

And so by September 1, according to the figures given by Georg W. Feuchter in his excellent book *Der Luftkrieg,* Bomber

Air-Marshal Sir Arthur 'Bomber' Harris, born in 1892, firmly believed in the decisiveness of air power. From February 1942 he directed R.A.F. Bomber Command in its onslaught on Germany. He deployed all available aircraft in the first 1,000-bomber raid on Cologne on May 30, 1942, devastating one-third of the city. In September 1942, the first 8,000-lb 'blockbuster' bomb was dropped on Karlsruhe. He initiated night bombing to supplement day raids, and introduced area bombing.

The Avro Lancaster was built in greater numbers than any other British four-engined bomber of World War II, a total of 7,374 being produced. Derived from the twin-engined Manchester, whose performance had been good, but whose engines proved totally unreliable, the Merlin-engined Lancaster first appeared in 1941. It proved an excellent aircraft, capable of carrying enormous loads, and very easy to fly. Besides large loads of conventional bombs, the Lancaster could carry such special stores as "Dambuster" bombs, 12,000-lb "Tallboys" and 22,000-lb "Grand Slams". Its one major failing was lack of ventral protection.
◁ *In flight.*
▽ *A Bomber Command station with Lancasters at their dispersal points.*
▷ *Bombing up.*
▷ ▷ *Aircrew.*
▷ ▽ *Maintenance.*
▷ ▽ ▽ *Debriefing.*

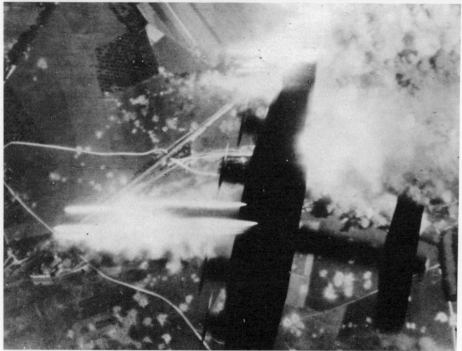

△ △ *The pilot runs up his Lancaster's engines before taking off for a night mission.*
△ *A Halifax silhouetted over the target area by the flares, bomb-bursts, and fires below.*

of the German Foreign Office, were lost without trace.

9,000 tons on Hamburg

During the last week in July, Hamburg and its port were reduced to ruins by the concerted efforts of Bomber Command and the 8th Air Force, a combined operation unique of its kind. The operation was called "Gomorrah" and started on the evening of July 24 with an enormous release of "Window". To follow the effect of this decoy device, let us go with Cajus Bekker to Stade on the lower Elbe and into the command post where Lieutenant-General Schwabedissen was about to send up the fighters of his 2nd *Fliegerdivision*:

"But on this July 24 the inconceivable took place. It was shortly before midnight when the first reports reached Stade, and the projections on the screen showed the enemy bomber formations flying eastwards over the North Sea, parallel to the coast. The Bf 110's of NJG [*Nachtjagdgeschwader*] 3 were duly ordered off from their bases at Stade, Vechta, Wittmundhaven, Wunstorf, Lüneburg and Kastrup, and took up their positions over the sea under *"Himmelbett"* control. Meanwhile it was confirmed that the initial Pathfinders were being followed by a bomber stream of several hundred aircraft, all keeping to the north of the Elbe estuary. What was their objective? Would they turn south to Kiel or Lübeck, or proceed over the Baltic for some target as yet

Command had attacked the following German cities with the amounts of bombs shown over the previous eight months:

	tons		tons
Hamburg	11,000	Berlin	6,000
Essen	8,000	Dusseldorf	5,000
Duisburg	6,000	Nuremberg	5,000

The massive attacks on the capital of the Third Reich began again on November 18 and between that date and January 1, 1944 no less than 14,000 tons of bombs transformed it into an immense heap of rubble. It was during this period that the archives of the French G.H.Q., discovered in the station at La Charité-sur-Loire on June 19, 1940 by the 9th Panzer Division and then preserved in an annexe

The British Avro Lancaster B. I heavy bomber

Engines: four Rolls-Royce Merlin XXII inlines, 1,460-hp each.
Armament: eight .303-inch Browning machine guns and up to 18,000 lbs of bombs.
Speed: 287 mph at 11,500 feet.
Ceiling: 24,500 feet.
Range: 2,530 miles with 7,000-lb bomb-load, 1,730 miles with 12,000-lb.
Weight empty/loaded: 36,900/68,000 lbs.
Span: 102 feet.
Length: 69 feet 6 inches.
Height: 20 feet 6 inches.
Crew: 7.

THE DAMBUSTERS

The famous "Dams Raid" of May 16, 1943 was intended to breach the Möhne (right), Eder, Sorpe, Lister, and Schwelme dams. Converted Lancasters of 617 Squadron (top) attacked with special bombs designed by Mr. Barnes Wallis (above) which, when released at a precise speed and height, skipped over the dams' net defences and rolled down the inside wall of the dam to explode at a predetermined depth. The shock wave then caused the dam to break. The Schwelme dam was not attacked, and only the Möhne and Eder dams were breached.

△ △ ◁ Water pours through the gap in the Eder dam, causing severe, but only local, damage to agricultural land.

△ △▷ The last of the water held back by the Möhne dam streams through the breach.

△ Below the Möhne dam: the flood waters spread over the river valley. But only if all five targets had been destroyed would German industry have felt any long-term effects.

◁ Wing-Commander Guy Gibson, V.C. (centre), commander of 617 Squadron.

▷ The King, with Gibson looking over his shoulder, inspects photographs of the results.

The de Havilland Mosquito, of laminated wood construction, was one of the most versatile aircraft to see service in the war. It served as a bomber, fighter-bomber, reconnaissance aircraft, night fighter, strike fighter, and in several other rôles. Illustrated are aircraft of 139 Squadron.

unknown? All now depended on closely following their course without being deceived by any feint attack.

"Suddenly the Stade operations room throbbed with disquietude. For minutes the illuminations on the screen representing the enemy had stuck in the same positions. The signals officer switched in to the direct lines to the radar stations and asked what was the matter. He received the same answer from all of them: 'Apparatus put out of action by jamming.'

"The whole thing was a mystery. Then came reports from the 'Freya' stations, operating on the long 240-cm wave, that they too were jammed. They at least could just distinguish the bomber formation's echo from the artificial ones. But the screens of the 'Würzburgs', operating on 53-cm, became an indecipherable jumble of echo points resembling giant insects, from which nothing could be recognised at all.

"It was a portentous situation, for the control of the night fighters entirely depended on exact information as to position and altitude being given by the 'Würzburgs'. Without it the controllers were powerless and the fighters could only fumble in the dark.

"2nd *Fliegerdivision* had to turn for help to the general air-raid warning system—to the corps of observers watching and listening throughout the land. These could only report what they saw. At Dithmarschen, not far from Meldorf, they saw yellow lights cascading from the sky; more and more of them all in the same area. Presumably they marked a turning point. The bomber stream had veered to the south-east, as fresh reports confirmed. In close order the enemy was heading parallel with the Elbe—direct to Hamburg."

Similarly handicapped, the 54 batteries of heavy (8.8-cm) A.A. and the 26 batteries of light A.A. defending the great city of Hamburg could only fire in barrage. They thus claimed only 12 victims out of the 374 Lancasters, 246 Halifaxes, 125 Stirlings, and 73 Wellingtons which had taken off that evening, 721 of which reached their objective. On the following morning 235 Flying Fortresses took over from their R.A.F. comrades and on the 26th started their attacks again, concentrating their efforts on the shipyards and port installations. During the night of the 27th-28th Air Chief-Marshal Harris sent up 722 four-engined bombers against Hamburg

and 48 hours later another 699. As weather conditions had deteriorated, only 340 reached their objective during the night of August 2-3. During these six attacks nearly 3,000 British and American planes dropped 9,000 tons of bombs. In the resulting holocaust half the city was devoured by flames which ravaged 277,330 dwellings. Civilian victims totalled some 38,142 men, women, and children. All this was achieved at the cost of 89 British bombers shot down by fighters and A.A. These losses were light, of course, but this was not always to be the case for Bomber Command. In fact, between March 1 and July 1, 1943 the night attacks on the industrial complex of the Ruhr, when 18,506 sorties were made, cost 822 four-engined bombers and 5,600 crew. Replacements at the right time were not always easy, in spite of the efforts of the Dominions and the Allied powers.

A British success: the Mosquito

For its day operations over the Reich, which consisted of harassment or diversionary raids, the R.A.F. used principally the de Havilland Mosquito. Constructed almost entirely of wood, in which the firm had considerable experience, it was nevertheless one of the most successful of all the weapons which left British workshops. It weighed nine tons on take-off and its two motors delivered 2,500 hp, giving it a top speed of 400 mph, thus putting it virtually out of reach of enemy fighters. The Mosquitoes took part in 1,000 raids in 1943, attacking 40 German towns, including Berlin 27 times.

Hitler paralyses German reaction

When Hitler heard from Colonel Christian, his Luftwaffe A.D.C., about the first attack on Hamburg, he poured recrimination on the Luftwaffe for its shortcomings. From the shorthand transcript of this interminable indictment we quote only one passage, significant however in the way it reveals the way of thinking and reasoning of the master of

Air Chief-Marshal Sir C. Portal was born in 1893 and was head of Bomber Command in 1939 before becoming Chief of Air Staff in 1940. As such he realised that Bomber Command would have to play an important part in the war before the Allies could invade the continent, and laid the foundations of its expansion well. He was greatly respected by the Americans and had great influence at all conferences.

Lieutenant-General James R. Doolittle was born in 1896, and first came to prominence with the "Doolittle Raid" on Japan in April 1942. Later that year he commanded the 12th Air Force in the "Torch" operations, and in 1943 the Strategic Air Forces operating against Italy. During August he led a major raid on Rome. In 1944 he assumed command of the 8th Air Force in Britain, and later commanded U.S. air forces in the Pacific. Between the wars Doolittle had been a record breaker, and was the only non-regular officer to command a major air force in combat.

▵ *A German town begins to burn. By now the boot was firmly on the other foot, and with the arrival of the 8th Air Force in Europe the Allied bombing offensive would go from strength to strength.*

▷ *Ruins in Nuremberg, one of the Nazi party's spiritual homes, devastated by an Allied raid.*

enough planes!' well, we have enough to do other things than what we are doing. On another occasion someone said: 'It wouldn't have the effect we want anyway,' and then he added: 'We must sow mines,' and another time: 'The A.A. was very heavy' and the next day: 'The A.A. fire was no good!' Most of what I hear all the time means: 'We can't find our objective'. Not to find London, that's shameful! And then I have to hear some idiot tell me: 'Yes, *mein Führer,* when the British planes come over Dortmund with their ray-guided bomb-aimers they can drop their bombs precisely on blocks of buildings 500 yards wide and 250 yards long.' Fool! But we can't even find London which is 35 miles across and less than 100 miles from the coast! That's what I told those gentlemen. I'm not saying this for your benefit Christian. You can't do anything about it. You're an A.D.C. I'm saying it also for other interested persons."

As we can see, Hitler accused the Luftwaffe of "beating about the bush" when he had asked for reprisals against English cities. Shortly before this he had said to Christian: "You can only break terror with terror. We must get to counter-attack; everything else is folly."

But how could the *Reichsmarschall* counter-attack with the means then at his disposal? The fear of a raid on London by 50 two-engined bombers was not

△ *A German air raid poster exhorts the civilian population to watch out for shell splinters from A.A. fire.*

▽ *Focke-Wulf 190 line-up. With later models of the Bf 109, this superb fighter formed the backbone of the Luftwaffe's day fighter force.*

the Third Reich: "That they should attack our aerodromes, I care little; but when they demolish the cities of the Ruhr! And they [the British] are very easily upset: a few bombs filled with the new explosives soon put the wind up them. 'The Germans have got a new weapon!' I don't know why we're beating about the bush here in Germany. The only way to stop this is to impress those on the other side; otherwise people will go mad here. In time things will come to such a pass that they will lose all confidence in the Luftwaffe. Anyway that confidence is partly gone already. Then you can't come and say 'We've laid mines in the enemy's waters!' For whether he comes over Hamburg with 400 to 500 planes, or only 200 to 300 it's all the same. But look at us dithering about! The only way we can make any impression is ourselves to bomb the towns on the other side methodically. But when I hear people say: 'We didn't find our objective,' and then the next time: 'We haven't got

likely to put Harris off sending 700 or 800 four-engined bombers over Berlin the next day. Hitler's grievance was thus imaginary. But for all that, the high-ranking officers of the Luftwaffe were not without blame, though Hitler in his diatribe did not touch on the real reason: the failure to take advantage of the brilliant team of scientists and technologists then working in Germany on jet and rocket propulsion.

The aircraft manufacturer Ernst Heinkel had prospected in both these directions as early as 1935 with the collaboration of the young Wernher von Braun in the field of the rocket and of the engineer

△ △ *A stick of bombs starts its long fall into Germany.*
△ *A B-24 Liberator heads for home over the Luftwaffe airfield at Saint-Didier. The airfield itself (centre right) seems relatively undamaged, but the administrative buildings (top right) and dispersal areas (bottom centre) appear to have been hit severely.*

Pabst von Ohain in that of the turbojet. The rocket-powered Heinkel 176, using a liquid propellant, was the first to be ready and it was demonstrated to Hitler, who was accompanied by Generals Göring, Milch, Jeschonnek, and Udet of the Luftwaffe, on July 3, 1939 by test pilot Erich Warsitz. On the following August 27, three years ahead of the British Frank Whittle's plane of the same type, the Heinkel 178, the first jet aeroplane in the world, took off from a landing strip near Berlin. On October 27, 1939, in the absence of Göring, who could not be bothered to attend, it was seen by Secretary of State Milch and General Udet, who were not impressed.

The idea was taken up again by Messerschmitt and on July 26, 1943 Major-General Adolf Galland, who in the previous year at the age of 30 had been appointed head of the German Fighter Command, was invited by the makers to fly the twin-

engined jet propelled Me 262. "It's like being driven by an angel," he said when questioned on his impressions after the test flight, but in his memoirs he added: "On landing I was more enthusiastic than I had ever been before. Feelings and impressions were, however, no criterion; it was the performance and characteristics that mattered. This was not a step forward, this was a leap!"

In fact the Messerschmitt Me 262 could do 540 mph in level flight, twice the speed, that is, of the British and American four-engined bombers. It could climb at record speed, had a range of 50-70 minutes' flying time, and used low-grade fuel.

Was Germany going to have another chance, then, after the inconceivable indifference shown by Göring, Milch, Jeschonnek, and Udet towards Heinkel's revolutionary plane? Evidently not, for at the first demonstration of Messerschmitt's pure-bred interceptor Hitler demanded that it be changed into a fighter-bomber. And in what terms! "For years," he said in front of Göring, Galland, and Messerschmitt, "I have demanded from the Luftwaffe a Speed Bomber which can reach its target in spite of enemy defence. In this aircraft you present me as a fighter plane I see the *Blitz* Bomber, with which I will repel the Invasion in its first and weakest phase. Regardless of the enemy's air umbrella, it will strike the recently landed mass of material and troops, creating panic, death and destruction. *At last this is the Blitz Bomber!* Of course none of you thought of that.'"

This meant a whole series of modifications to the prototype, listed by Bekker thus:

"Bombs would make the take-off weight too heavy for the slender legs. Undercarriage and tyres had to be reinforced. For bombing missions the range was inadequate, so auxiliary tanks had to be built in. That displaced the centre of gravity, upsetting the plane's stability. No approved method of bomb-suspension, nor even a bomb-sight, existed for such a plane, and the normal fighter reflector-sight bombs could only be aimed in a shallow angle of dive. For regular dive-bombing the machine was too fast safely to hold on target. An order from Führer H.Q. expressly forbade such dives—or indeed any speed exceeding 470 m.p.h."

And so, instead of taking part in the defence of the skies over Germany from 1943-1944, the redoubtable Messerschmitt

The American Consolidated B-24J Liberator heavy bomber

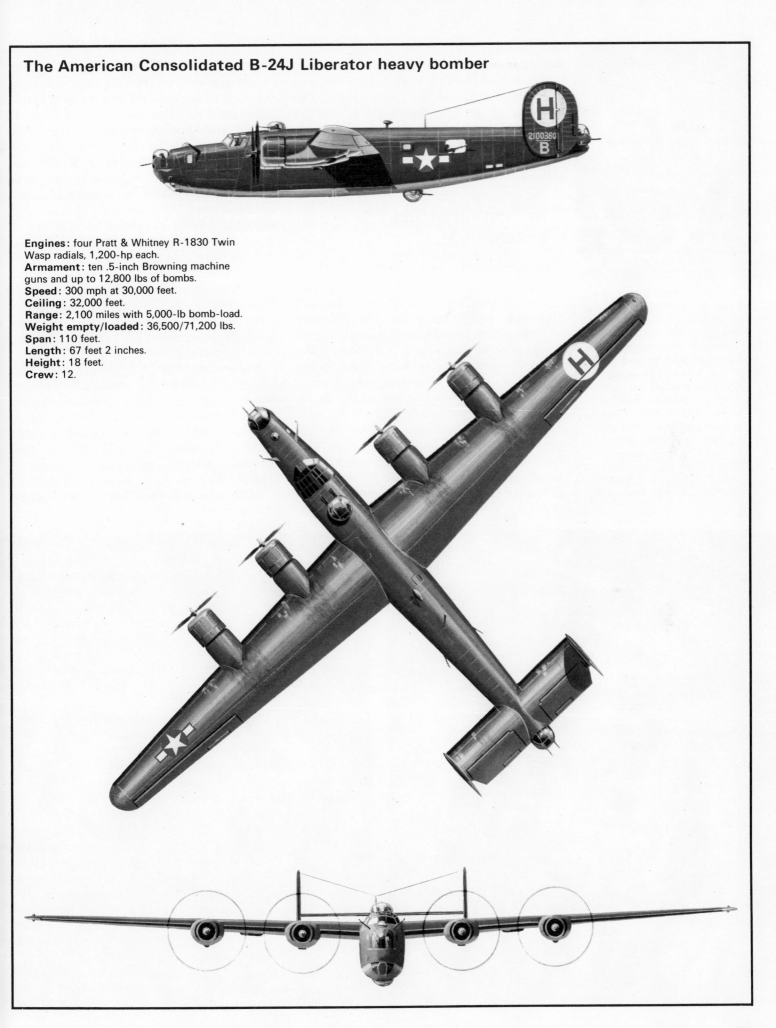

Engines: four Pratt & Whitney R-1830 Twin
Wasp radials, 1,200-hp each.
Armament: ten .5-inch Browning machine
guns and up to 12,800 lbs of bombs.
Speed: 300 mph at 30,000 feet.
Ceiling: 32,000 feet.
Range: 2,100 miles with 5,000-lb bomb-load.
Weight empty/loaded: 36,500/71,200 lbs.
Span: 110 feet.
Length: 67 feet 2 inches.
Height: 18 feet.
Crew: 12.

Me 262 failed to turn up over the beaches assigned to it by Hitler. It was first seen over the Albert Canal when it was reported in Allied communiqués at the beginning of September 1944. Yet in spite of this disastrous delay it came into use eight months before its R.A.F. counterpart, the Gloster Meteor, the first Allied plane of this type.

The British attack Peenemünde

"Break terror by terror." When Hitler had said this on July 25, 1943 he was thinking not merely of the counter-attacks which he was demanding from the Luftwaffe, but especially of the retaliatory weapons which were then being perfected at the Peenemünde testing station on the shores of the Baltic under the command of General Walter Dornberger. Since January 1943 the Allies' secret services had been on the alert for a new enemy weapon which French resistance agents were calling the "self-propelled shell". In his memoirs Churchill reports certain boasts which Hitler made about this weapon to reassure his entourage:

"By the end of 1943 London would be levelled to the ground and Britain forced to capitulate. October 20 was fixed as zero day for rocket attacks to begin. It is said that Hitler personally ordered the construction of 30,000 rockets for that day. This, if true, shows the absurd ideas on which he lived. The German Minister of Munitions, Dr. Speer, said that each V2 required about as many man-hours to make as six fighters. Hitler's demand was therefore for the equivalent of 180,000 fighters to be made in four months. This was ridiculous; but the production of both weapons was given first priority and 1,500 skilled workers were transferred from anti-aircraft and artillery production to the task."

As the threat grew more real, the Prime Minister charged his son-in-law Duncan Sandys with the task of centralising all work connected with rockets, their characteristics, their manufacture, and their installation, as well as the best methods of fighting them. On June 11 Duncan Sandys wrote to Churchill:

"The latest air reconnaissance photographs provide evidence that the Germans

Wernher von Braun was born in 1912, and was one of Germany's ablest rocket engineers. Braun became the Technical Director of the German Army's rocket research centre at Peenemünde in 1937. Though great progress on missiles had been made by 1940, Hitler's interference seriously hampered further advances. He was arrested by the Gestapo but released on Hitler's express orders. Operations with V-2s started in September 1944.

are pressing on as quickly as possible with the development of the long-range rocket at the experimental establishment at Peenemünde, and that frequent firings are taking place. There are also signs that the light anti-aircraft defences at Peenemünde are being further strengthened.

"In these circumstances it is desirable that the projected bombing attack upon this establishment should be proceeded with as soon as possible."

The raid recommended in these terms was carried out during the night of August 16-17 by 597 four-engined bombers of Bomber Command which were ordered to drop 1,500 tons of high explosive and incendiaries from the then unusual height of just over 8,000 feet. On take-off the pilots were warned that in case of failure they would begin again without regard to the losses sustained or about to be sustained. The operation was carried out with magnificent dash and spirit and without excessive losses, a diversionary raid on Berlin having drawn off most of the German fighters. At the time the Anglo-American propaganda no doubt exaggerated the results of the raids, yet the operation did appreciably slow down the German V-1 and V-2 programme which, according to Hitler, was going to bring Britain to face the alternative of annihilation or capitulation before the end of the year. It was in fact on the eighth day of Operation "Overlord", that is only on June 13, 1944, that the first V-1 flying bomb took off for London.

The results

Altogether, 135,000 tons of bombs were dropped on Germany between January 1 and December 31, 1943. With what result? As we have seen, following the proclamation of full mobilisation as a consequence of Stalingrad, German war production shattered all records in every variety of weapon. And, in spite of fearful suffering, the morale of the German people was not badly affected by this pitiless offensive.

This is not to say that, accurate though these statements are, the Anglo-American offensive was a failure. On this point Georg Feuchter, in his *Der Luftkrieg,* makes two valuable observations.

The first concerns the ever-increasing ratio of A.A. weapons being made within the German armament industry. This eventually reached first 20 per cent and then 30 per cent of all artillery and brought with it a corresponding inflation in guncrews. In 1942 these amounted to 439,000 men, in 1943 there were 600,000, and there were nearly 900,000 in 1944. The increase was achieved at the expense of the Eastern Front where there were virtually none left. The second observation is equally, if not more, important. The German war industry owed its survival to a system of extreme decentralisation. The maintenance of its production depended in the last resort on keeping open the railways, the rivers, and the roads. On the day when the Anglo-Americans shifted the centre of gravity of their operations to the communications within the Third Reich, Dr. Speer's already overstretched network began rapidly to disintegrate and, once started, this became irreversible. The two Western Allies no longer lacked the means. At the end of the year Lieutenant-General Ira C. Eaker, from whom his colleague James H. Doolittle had taken over in Great Britain, assumed command of the 15th Air Force, a large new American strategic bombing formation.

◁▽ Peenemünde before and after the Allied visitation on August 16-17. Damage to German installations was heavy, but of the 597 British bombers despatched, 40 failed to return and 32 others were damaged.
▽ Germany learns the horrors of the area bombing so beloved by "Bomber" Harris.
Overleaf: Getting ready for the fray. Staff Sergeant Lusic of the 8th Air Force shows the preparations needed by an air gunner before he even boards his aircraft.

CHAPTER 115
Eisenhower's build-up

Let us cross the Channel and watch the preparations for "Overlord" from London. S.H.A.E.F. (Supreme Headquarters Allied Expeditionary Forces) had been set up under the initiative and the control of the Combined Chiefs-of-Staff Committee. In fact, it did not function with absolute smoothness but it should be noted that, with a few exceptions, the disagreements were not manifest during the preparation period. And up to mid-July 1944, Generals Eisenhower and Montgomery did really work shoulder to shoulder, though the functions that Montgomery took on himself did lead to some misunderstanding and were not understood in the same way by both men.

Writing to General Marshall on this matter on December 23, 1943, Eisenhower expressed his views as follows:

"In the early stages of OVERLORD I see no necessity for British and American Army Group Commanders. In fact, any such setup would be destructive of the essential co-ordination between Ground and Air Forces."

Consequently, he entrusted Montgomery with the command of British and American land forces taking part in the landing itself and in later operations designed to consolidate and then extend the bridgeheads. Therefore Montgomery would have the responsibility of preparing and leading to its conclusion the offensive which would seal the fate of the German armies engaged in Normandy.

But later, when the Allies were out of Normandy, the victory would be exploited and this would take the Grand Alliance right to the very heart of Germany. This would be preceded by the establishment of two army groups, one Anglo-Canadian and the other American.

Montgomery would assume command of the first and Bradley was called upon to lead the second. Eisenhower would once more take over the command of land operations and remain C.-in-C.

△ "Somewhere in England"– the men of an American artillery unit rest by the roadside during the great build-up of the "Overlord" forces in southern England.

1597

Nothing, in the documents we have, indicates that Eisenhower left Montgomery under any misconception about his intention of taking over the reins from him again, but everything goes to prove that, in his heart of hearts, Montgomery had flattered himself that his superior would change his mind in view of the successes that he (Montgomery) would win for him, and that, until the final victory, Eisenhower would leave him as commander of land forces which he had entrusted to him for the first stages of Operation "Overlord". But Eisenhower had had a taste of ambitious subordinates, in the person of the amiable General Sir Harold Alexander, and he was not inclined to experience it again. Even if he had resigned himself to playing the rôle of a figurehead, his powerful American subordinates would not have put up with it, nor would his superior General George C. Marshall, and much less still American public opinion, which was influenced by a swarm of war correspondents accredited to S.H.A.E.F. The least that can be said about them is that

they were not very responsive to their British ally's point of view or methods.

British opinions of Eisenhower

But furthermore, and perhaps this is the most important point, it must be noted that, rightly or wrongly, General Eisenhower's personality did not greatly impress Montgomery. The latter had a real superiority complex in matters of strategy towards his chief. But Montgomery was not the only general in the British hierarchy who felt like this in regard to the American supreme commander. On May 15, 1944, leaving a conference during which Eisenhower, together with his subordinates, had explained his operational plans in the presence of George VI, the Prime Minister, and Field-Marshal Smuts, Brooke noted in his diary:

"The main impression I gathered was that Eisenhower was no real director of thought, plans, energy or direction. Just a co-ordinator, a good mixer, a champion of inter-Allied co-operation, and in those respects few can hold the candle to him. But is that enough? Or can we not find all qualities of a commander in one man? May be I am getting too hard to please, but I doubt it."

Re-reading his notes two years later, Lord Alanbrooke changes this portrait only in tone. This is how he depicts him:

"A past-master in the handling of allies, entirely impartial and consequently trusted by all. A charming personality and good co-ordinator. But no real commander . . . Ike might have been a showman calling on various actors to perform their various turns, but he was not the commander of the show who controlled and directed all the actors."

Eisenhower's personality

Unlike Brooke, Montgomery, MacArthur, and Patton, Eisenhower had not taken part in World War I and the highest command he had ever had in the interwar years had been that of an infantry battalion. So, though he was completely at home with all aspects of staff work, he did not possess the tactical imagination which characterised to a rare degree

men such as Bradley and Montgomery. Certainly, though, he had a remarkable aptitude for assimilating the ideas of others and fitting them into the more general picture of his own sphere of responsibility.

In addition, there is much to admire in the calm authority, the tact, and the psychological deftness of a man who could get on with a subordinate as difficult as Montgomery, who, when asked, "But don't you ever obey orders?" could reply: "If I don't like them I'll go as far as I can in disobedience and try to bluff my way through. But, of course, if I can't get what I want, then I must submit in the end."

Likewise, Eisenhower managed to soften the verbal brutality of the brilliant but at times unbearable George S. Patton, at the same time as he promoted above his head the "serious, zealous and very cultivated" Omar N. Bradley, who had been Patton's subordinate in Sicily, without the least tension between these two soldiers of such great difference in temperament and method. The respect he had for them did not, nevertheless, prevent him from turning a deaf ear when some depreciatory remark about their British allies passed their lips.

It has been said that Eisenhower did not impose his will. It would be more accurate to say that he did not impose

◁△ British tank crews load their Shermans aboard landing-craft.
◁▽ Eisenhower (standing, with binoculars) and Tedder watch American tank men training.
△ A stockpile of gun wheels and artillery wheels in southern England.

▽ A mobile, swastika-bedecked target for anti-tank gunners on practice shoots.

△ The man who drew the first blueprints for "Overlord": C.O.S.S.A.C., short for "Chief-of-Staff to the Supreme Allied Commander". Lieutenant-General F. E. Morgan was given the post at the time of the Casablanca Conference.
▽ The final team, S.H.A.E.F.– "Supreme Headquarters of the Allied Expeditionary Forces". Left to right: Bradley, Ramsay, Tedder, Eisenhower, Montgomery, Leigh-Mallory, Bedell Smith.

himself often, but that he did so whenever the situation demanded his personal intervention, and then always very deliberately. Two examples will suffice to justify this point of view.

One week before the launching of "Overlord", Air Chief-Marshal Leigh-Mallory, commanding the tactical air forces, came for the last time to protest that a useless massacre awaited the American 82nd and 101st Airborne Divisions if the command insisted on landing them in the Cotentin peninsula. According to him, losses of glider-borne troops would amount to 70 per cent and half the paratroops would be killed or wounded in the drop. As Eisenhower himself later recorded: "I instructed the air commander to put his recommendations in a letter and informed him he would have my answer within a few hours."

After the few hours had passed, Eisenhower telephoned Leigh-Mallory. As the "Utah" Beach landing could not be abandoned, he was sticking to his deci-

sion, but he did not omit to tell Leigh-Mallory that his orders would be confirmed in writing. On December 19, 1944, with the Panzers advancing on Bastogne in the Ardennes, he would demonstrate the same characteristic *sang-froid* of a great leader. He had gone to Verdun, where he was awaited by Generals Bradley, Devers, and Patton. He said boldly as he opened the sitting: "The present situation is to be regarded as one of opportunity for us and not of disaster. There will be only cheerful faces at this conference table."

What is more, as his deputy he kept Air Chief-Marshal Sir Arthur Tedder, who had been attached in this capacity since the end of January 1943. Here he could count on a first class ally, particularly qualified to get him the unreserved support of the British strategic air forces. He also brought to S.H.A.E.F. his incomparable chief-of-staff, Lieutenant-General Bedell Smith who, according to Lord Alanbrooke, served him in the most

◁ Key weapon for the assault: the D.D. (Duplex Drive) swimming tank. The D.D. was a waterproofed Sherman with twin propellers driven by the tank's engine. It was supported in the water by a deep, collapsible skirt which was lowered on reaching the beach, enabling the gun to come into action at once while the drive was shifted from the propellers to the tank tracks. The D.D. was a classic example of the British adapting a proved American weapon to a specialist rôle. At Bradley's headquarters these novel weapons were viewed with scepticism – which was to have bloody results on "Omaha" Beach.
▽ American Shermans on field manoeuvres.

fortunate and efficient manner possible.

The C.O.S.S.A.C. plan criticised

On January 2, 1944 Eisenhower was received at the Pentagon, where he had been summoned by General Marshall, and then went to the bedside of President Roosevelt, who was incapacitated for a few days. He would willingly have foregone having to go so far out of his way on his journey from Tunis to London, for time was pressing and what he knew of the plan drawn up by Lieutenant-General Sir F. E. Morgan and the C.O.S.S.A.C. group (Chief-of-Staff Allied Supreme Commander) was only partly to his liking.

"I was doubtful about the adequacy of the tactical plan because it contemplated an amphibious attack on a relatively narrow, three-division front with a total of only five divisions afloat at the instant of assault . . . In addition to being disturbed by the constricted nature of the proposed manoeuvre, I was also concerned because the outline I had seen failed to provide effectively for the quick capture of Cherbourg. I was convinced that the plan, unless it had been changed since I had seen it, did not emphasize sufficiently the early need for major

ports and for rapid build-up."

Therefore, even before he flew off to the United States, he instructed Montgomery to get together with Bedell Smith and begin an analysis and, if necessary, a revision of the C.O.S.S.A.C. plan and to report to him on the results of this on his return to London in mid-January.

As soon as his eye fell on the documents submitted to him, Montgomery made up his mind. The plan was "impracticable". This abrupt opinion was based on the following considerations:

"The initial landing is on too narrow a front and is confined to too small an area.

"By D+12 a total of 16 divisions has been landed on the same beaches as were used for the initial landings. This would

continued on page 1608

▷ and ▽ Another example of
British specialised armour: the
"Crocodile", a flame-throwing
tank. The Crocodile consisted
of a Churchill tank with the
inflammable fuel for the
flame-thrower contained in a
small armoured trailer. The fuel
was pumped through the tank
to the nozzle by compressed
nitrogen. It was an impressive
and devastating weapon.

The British Churchill VII Crocodile flame-thrower tank

Weight: 41.2 tons.
Other specifications and performance figures: as for Churchill VII.
Flame-throwing equipment: the hull machine gun was replaced by the flame projector, which was fed from
the two-wheel trailer via the linkage between the trailer and tank and an armoured pipe under the belly of the
tank. The armoured trailer weighed 6.5 tons, and carried 400 gallons of flame fuel, enough for 80 one-second
bursts. The trailer could be jettisoned if hit, and the Churchill could then perform as an ordinary tank. The range
of the flame projector was between 80 and 120 yards.

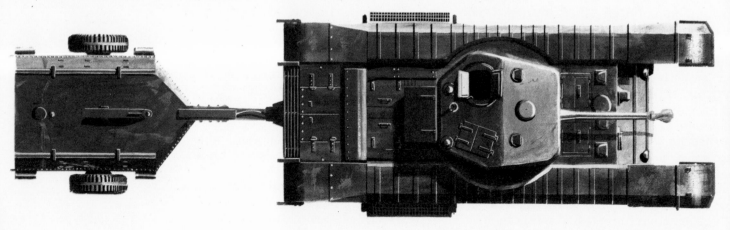

The British Infantry Tank Mark IV Churchill VII

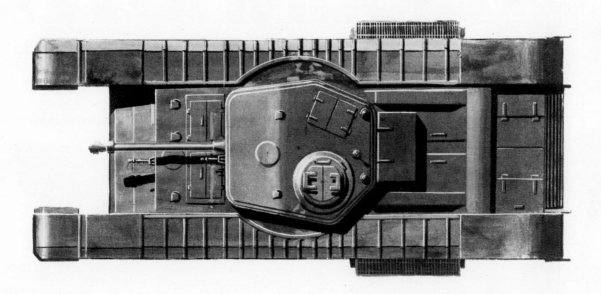

Weight: 40 tons.
Crew: 5.
Armament: one 75-mm Mark 5 gun with 84 rounds plus one .303-inch Bren and two 7.92-mm Besa machine guns with 600 and 6,525 rounds respectively.
Armour: hull front 152-mm, sides 95-mm, rear 50-mm, and decking 19-mm; turret front 152-mm, sides 94-mm, and roof 20-mm.
Engine: one Bedford "Twin-Six" 12-cylinder inline, 340-hp.
Speed: 13.5 mph.
Range: 90 miles.
Length: 24 feet 2 inches.
Width: 10 feet 10½ inches.
Height: 8 feet 10¼ inches.

EISENHOWER
ALLIED SUPREMO

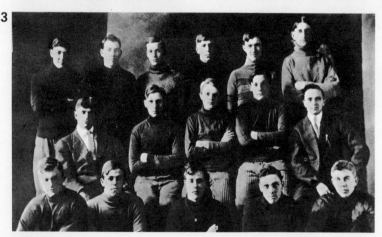

Dwight D. Eisenhower: Allied supreme commander, soldier, diplomat; figurehead of the Anglo-American victory in Europe–all summed up in the three letters which spell "Ike".

Eisenhower was born on October 14, 1890, at Denison, Texas, the third son of a poor and hard-working family. In 1911 he entered the West Point Military Academy and passed out in the top third of his class. He commanded a tank training centre during World War I and was promoted major after the war.

From 1922 to 1924 Eisenhower served in the Panama Canal Zone; and then, in 1926, he took the first important step up the ladder to high command, graduating from the U.S. Army's command and general staff school first out of a class of 275. In 1928 he added to his laurels by graduating from the Army War College. This was followed by a year in France, up-dating a guide-book to American battlefields. Subsequent posts in Washington, D.C., culminated in his appointment in 1933 to the office of the chief-of-staff of General MacArthur. When Mac-Arthur went to the Philippines in 1935 as military adviser, Eisen-

1. *Ike in the cockpit of a Marauder bomber.*
2. *At the age of two (lower right) with three of his brothers.*
3. *Member of the Abilene football team (back row, third from left).*
4. *Family reunion, 1926. Lieutenant-Colonel Eisenhower at left, standing.*
5. *Ike samples Army "C" rations in Tunisia.*
6. *Supreme commander. Watching manoeuvres with Montgomery.*

7

8

9

10

hower went with him.

When war broke out in September 1939 Eisenhower returned to the United States. In the summer manoeuvres in 1941 he made his mark as chief-of-staff of the 3rd Army and was soon promoted to brigadier-general. After Pearl Harbor he was recalled to Washington to serve as assistant chief of the war plans division of the general staff. This work naturally involved planning for the eventual invasion of Europe, which in turn required close discussion with the British, carried out by Eisenhower in April-May 1942. The following month Eisenhower returned to London as commander of the European Theatre of Operations (E.T.O.).

Eisenhower's baptism of fire in the E.T.O. was not a gentle one. In Algeria and Tunisia he had to co-ordinate the movements of the 1st and 8th Armies – and cope with Rommel's push at Kasserine. The Tunisian campaign, however, proved conclusively that he really did have the magic blend of talents which got the best out of his wildly differing subordinates while coping with the all-time incalculable factor in war: unexpected and dangerous moves by the enemy at the worst moment.

Eisenhower's next task was the conquest of Sicily. Here he had to co-ordinate the 7th and 8th Armies and the differing talents of Patton and Montgomery. He showed his firmness as the "man in charge" by his disciplining of Patton over the "slapping incident" – when Patton slapped soldiers whom he believed to be cowards. But Sicily was only the prelude to the negotiations for the surrender of Fascist Italy and the invasion of the Italian mainland.

Italian vacillation made these negotiations extremely tense, but Eisenhower finally tipped the scales by losing his temper. In the words of a British staff officer, he "demanded to be led to a telephone to speak to his Chief-of-Staff in Algiers. I took him to mine and waited while he bellowed down it, dictating on the spot a remarkably incisive telegram to be sent forthwith to Marshal Badoglio." This well-timed crack of the whip by Eisenhower had the desired effect and the surrender and landings both went ahead as planned.

The successful campaigns in Tunisia, Sicily, and Italy made Eisenhower an obvious contender for the supreme command of "Overlord"; but it took Roosevelt much soul-searching before he decided that the U.S. Army Chief-of-Staff, General Marshall, could not be spared from his current duties. The President made his decision on December 5, 1943. "Ike" would command the "Overlord" forces.

Eisenhower had formidable advantages when he took up his task. He had the fruits of all the preliminary work which had been put in on the subject. He had all the expert advice he needed, plus the knowledge that his forces would have technical and material superiority. And he had a sound team of subordinates. Yet all his tact and patience was still required to get those subordinates to give of their best – and at this "Ike" was a past master.

1

7. *With Mark Clark in London, returning a ranker's salute.*
8. *Chatting with paratroops.*
9. *The soldier-diplomat; Ike with the formidable combination of Churchill and de Gaulle.*
10. *Head of the S.H.A.E.F. team – with his hand on Berlin.*
11. *At a rubber dinghy demonstration.*
12. *Presenting a U.S. Army carbine to Montgomery.*
13. *A talk with the bomber chiefs – Brereton (left) and Spaatz.*
14. *Making a point on field manoeuvres.*
15. *Loneliness of command.*

2

3

5

14

△ and ▷ *Paratroops, who would form the airborne spearhead of the assault, in training. Heavy paratroop attacks were scheduled for both flanks of the invasion front.*

▽ *British airborne troops are given glider instruction.*

continued from page 1601

lead to the most appalling confusion on the beaches, and the smooth development of the land battle would be made extremely difficult—if not impossible.

"Further divisions come pouring in, all over the same beaches. By D+24 a total of 24 divisions have been landed, all over the same beaches; control of the beaches would be very difficult; the confusion, instead of getting better, would get worse."

It will be noted that the objections which Montgomery raised about the C.O.S.S.A.C. plan, which he submitted confidentially to Churchill, convalescing in Marrakesh at the time, were based on considerations different from Eisenhower's. Nevertheless, they reinforced his determination to throw the whole project back into the melting-pot when he returned to London on January 14.

Montgomery's views prevail

Here, as Montgomery was responsible for the landings and their initial advance,

How to lift an airborne division: Horsa gliders and Halifax and Stirling tugs.

he was not content with the severe analysis just quoted from, but proposed another plan. Considering only the land forces, Montgomery's memorandum concluded that the following points were vital:

"*(a)* The initial landings must be made on the widest possible front.

(b) Corps must be able to develop operations from their own beaches, and other corps must NOT land *through* those beaches.

(c) British and American areas of landing must be kept separate. The provisions of *(a)* above must apply in each case.

(d) After the initial landings, the operation must be developed in such a way that a good port is secured quickly for the British and for American forces. Each should have its own port or group of ports."

Having laid down these principles, which were eminently sensible, Montgomery proceeded to deduce from them a plan of operations, one of whose many merits was the inclusion of a properly co-ordinated plan for co-operation by the tactical and strategic air forces available:

"The type of plan required is on the following lines:

(a) One British army to land on a front of two, or possibly three, corps. One American army similarly.

(b) Follow-up divisions to come in to the corps already on shore.

(c) The available assault craft to be used for the landing troops. Successive flights to follow rapidly in any type of un-armoured craft, and to be poured in.

(d) The air battle must be won before the operation is launched. We must then aim at success in the land battle by the speed and violence of our operations."

Eisenhower agrees

General Eisenhower is to be praised for siding with his subordinate. And so the plan which was put into effect on June 6, 1944, was a very much amended form of the C.O.S.S.A.C. project:

1. The narrow front which had aroused criticism was widened to take in Saint Martin-de-Varreville ("Utah" Beach) on the right, and Lion-sur-Mer ("Sword" Beach), on the left.

2. The taking of a bridgehead on the eastern side of the Contentin peninsula

allowed the Allies to deal with the problem of Cherbourg at their ease and not to have to worry later about the serious obstacle presented by the River Vire.

3. Plan C.O.S.S.A.C. allowed for the initial landing of three divisions supported by a "floating reserve" against the 716th and 352nd Infantry Divisions of the German LXXXIV Corps. On the day that "Overlord" began, there were eight Allied divisions facing four German divisions. Moreover, in the "Utah" sector, the 91st and 709th Divisions would only be engaged in part. In addition, the second stage of the landing had been increased to include seven divisions.

From all this, should it be concluded

that Sir Frederick Morgan and the staff of C.O.S.S.A.C. had not looked far enough ahead and had come up with a plan which was too narrow and unambitious? If this is the conclusion, it can only be reached if one does not know that they were caught in an impossible situation.

Operation "Anvil", which, according to the decision of the Combined British and American Chiefs-of-Staff, confirmed by the Teheran Conference, was to precede "Overlord" and retain considerable quantities of landing equipment in the Western Mediterranean.

That is why on February 21, Montgomery wrote to Eisenhower: "I recommend very strongly that we now throw the whole weight of our opinion into the scales against ANVIL."

"Anvil" postponed

For strictly strategic reasons, Eisenhower refused to accept this point of view, for the mission which had been entrusted to him had read:

"You will enter the Continent of Europe and, in conjunction with the other Allied Nations, undertake operations aimed at the heart of Germany and the destruction of her Armed Forces."

This instruction seemed to Eisenhower to demand an advance up the valleys of the Rhône and the Saône, linking up somewhere in France with the right wing of the armies which had crossed the Channel. Nevertheless, he gave in to the argument that the success of "Overlord" could only be assured by the postponement of "Anvil" until after July 15.

"Overlord" put back to June

However, the alterations which came with the re-shaping of the C.O.S.S.A.C. plan forced the initial landing date to be put back from early May to early June. The actual date was subject to these considerations:

1. The parachute drop at night on both flanks of the attacking front required a date as close as possible to the full moon.
2. As three airborne divisions would be in action from midnight onwards, they

◁△ and ◁ *British engineers train in the building of pontoon bridges.*
△△ *"Wasps" (top), which were flame-throwing Bren-gun carriers, and a standard infantry flame-thrower.*
△ *More flame-thrower support for the "poor bloody infantry".*

had to be supported as soon as possible. Between dawn and the landing, a small interval of time would, nevertheless, be left free for the air forces and warships to neutralise and saturate the enemy's coastal defences.

3. Rommel's energetic multiplication of the quantity of mined obstructions on the beaches made it essential that Allied troops should reach them while the tide was still low enough not to have covered them, in order that the sappers in the first wave might have the utmost opportunity of dealing with the danger.

All these elements taken together timed the mighty enterprise within the dates of June 5 and June 7. It is worth noting in this connection that the Germans were taken unawares, for at every level of the Wehrmacht's hierarchy (Army Group "B", O.B.W., and O.K.W.), all were agreed that the invasion would be launched on the morning tide.

Eisenhower could not conceive of any later date for the landing which would not bring the whole Allied cause into serious danger. From the reports of his Intelligence network and from photographic reconnaissance, it appeared that there was a great increase in the number of launching ramps under construction in the Pas-de-Calais and the Cotentin peninsula, and that, within a few weeks, England would come under a new type of Blitz. Moreover the information he

1612

received from the U.S.A. concerning the advanced stage of development reached by bacteriological and atomic weapons encouraged him to make haste, because there was, of course, no guarantee that German science was not working in the same direction.

Montgomery's plan

In his memoirs, which appeared in 1958, Lord Montgomery explains his plan of attack:

"It is important to understand that, once we had secured a good footing in Normandy, my plan was to *threaten* to break out on the eastern flank, that is in the Caen sector. By pursuing this threat relentlessly I intended to draw the main enemy reserves, particularly his armoured divisions, into that sector and to keep them there – using the British and Canadian forces under Dempsey for this purpose. Having got the main enemy strength committed on the *eastern* flank, my plan was to make the break-out on the *western* flank – using for this task the

△ *This is the enemy – American troops are briefed on German uniform recognition. The photograph is a typical example of pre-D-Day security measures; the background of this picture has been erased.*
▷ *Fighters roll through an English town. Security again: not only the street name but the tram number and the name of the city transport corporation have been removed.*
▷▷ △ *Armour aboard ship. The tank in the centre is an "Ark", carrying a box-girder bridge for dropping over anti-tank ditches.*
▷▷ *Heavily camouflaged against prying German air reconnaissance: Allied trucks in an open field.*

American forces under General Bradley. This break-out attack was to be launched southwards, and then to proceed eastwards in a wide sweep up to the Seine about Paris. I hoped that this gigantic wheel would pivot on Falaise. It aimed to cut off all the enemy forces south of the Seine, the bridges over the river having been destroyed by our air forces."

Some critics have said that as Montgomery was writing after the war, he was constructing long-term aims of which he was not thinking at the time, so that he could say that Rommel had been forced to dance to his tune in France as well as in North Africa.

Martin Blumenson, one of the contributors to the monumental *U.S. Army in World War II,* put the question in this way in 1963:

"Did Montgomery, from the beginning of the invasion, plan to attract and contain the bulk of the German power to facilitate an American advance on the right? Or did he develop the plan later as a rationalisation for his failure to advance through Caen? Was he more concerned with conserving the limited British manpower and was his containment of the enemy therefore a brilliant expedient that emerged from the tactical situation in June? The questions were interesting but irrelevant, for the Germans had massed their power opposite the British without regard for General Montgomery's original intentions."

Questions like these are not idle, for other great captains, notably Napoleon and the older Moltke, have posed for posterity by remodelling their victories in order to attribute their successes to long and brilliant preparation, when really they were due to their facility for improvisation, and, in a situation which upset their careful calculations, to their aptitude for taking maximum advantage of the smallest favourable circumstances. In this argument, we do not hesitate to come down on the side of Lord Montgomery, and this can be proved with the aid of three texts contemporary with the events. They come from Sir Arthur Bryant's *Triumph in the West* which clothes, as it were, Brooke's daily notes:

1. On June 15, 1944 Montgomery wrote to Brooke: "When 2nd Panzer Division suddenly appeared in the Villers-Bocage–Caumont area, it plugged the hole through which I had broken. I think it had been meant for offensive action against I Corps in the Caen area. So long as

Rommel uses his strategic reserves to plug holes, that is good."

2. On June 18, Brooke noted, from a message sent by Montgomery to his army commanders: "Once we can capture Caen and Cherbourg and all face in the same direction we have a mighty chance—to make the German Army come to our threat and defeat it between the Seine and the Loire."

3. On June 27 Montgomery wrote to Brooke: "My general broad plan is maturing . . . All the decent enemy stuff, and his Pz. and Pz. S.S. divisions are coming in on the Second Army front—according to plan. That had made it much easier for the First U.S. Army to do its task."

The case seems proved.

Air power's rôle

The British and American strategic and tactical air forces were a vital element in the success of Operation "Overlord", after five months of intensive training.

For this purpose, General Eisenhower

△ *A group pose for G.I.s on the quayside.*
▷ *Embarkation drill in full kit. Barrage balloons for the invasion fleet in the background.*
▽ *Formation manoeuvres in landing-craft.*

had managed to have all strategic bomber formations, based in Great Britain and southern Italy, placed at his disposal. Under the immediate command of Lieutenant-General Carl A. Spaatz, they comprised:

1. R.A.F. Bomber Command (Air Chief-Marshal A. T. Harris);
2. The American 8th Air Force (Lieutenant-General James H. Doolittle) in Britain; and
3. The American 15th Air Force (Lieutenant-General Nathan F. Twining) in Italy.

In addition, through Air Chief-Marshal Leigh-Mallory, he was able to use the American 9th Air Force (Major-General Hoyt S. Vandenberg), and the British 2nd Tactical Air Force (Air-Marshal Sir Arthur Coningham).

For this air assault, American industry smashed all previous records. Between 1942 and 1943, its annual production had gone up from 48,000 to 86,000 machines of all types, until it reached a daily average of 350 in February 1944, i.e. close to one aeroplane every four minutes.

For its part, the R.A.F. had received 28,000 aircraft in 1943, of which 4,614 were four-engined bombers, 3,113 two-engined bombers, and 10,727 fighters and fighter-bombers. But by then British industry was working to its limit.

As regards the bombing of Germany, the division of labour between the British and the Americans worked according to a system established in 1943. Nevertheless, though Air Chief-Marshal Harris stuck obstinately to his theory that the Third Reich could be forced into defeat merely by the effects of strategic bombing, General H. H. Arnold, commanding the U.S. Army Air Force, saw another objective for the daytime raids of his Flying Fortresses and Liberators, escorted further and further into the heart of Germany by ever-increasing numbers of long-range fighters.

The idea was to force Göring's fighters to stretch themselves to the limit to defend the Reich's centres of industrial production and to destroy them there. Thus total mastery of the air would be gained, and this would guarantee success for the troops who were preparing to cross the Channel and invade the continent.

▽ *Battle training. This particular assault course consists of a 200-yard obstacle race with rifle and pack, to be covered in four minutes. Overleaf: A fair cross-section of the tools for the assault: tank and infantry landing-craft, and landing-ships in the background.*

CHAPTER 116
On the brink

In the space available it is not possible to present a complete picture of the operations carried out by the British and American strategic air forces against the German industrial machine. The following is a summing-up of these operations and an analysis of the results achieved.

On January 11, some 720 four-engined bombers of the 8th Air Force, forming a column of more than 200 miles long, shared between them the targets of Halberstadt, Braunschweig, Magdeburg, and Oschersleben. During the battles in the Westphalian sky, no less than 59 American bombers were shot down. It would still have been a great success if 152 German aircraft had shared the same fate, as was announced by General Doolittle's headquarters. However, it was learnt after the war that the Luftwaffe's losses that day were no more than 40 aircraft.

United States airmen refer to the week of February 20 to February 26 as the "Big Week". For seven days the 8th and 15th Air Forces, relieved at night by R.A.F. Bomber Command, concentrated on the German aircraft industry. In a

report to Stimson on February 27, 1945, General Arnold declared:

"The week of February 20-26, 1944 may well be classed by future historians as marking a decisive battle of history, one as decisive and of greater world importance than Gettysburg."

After calm appraisal, though, the historian cannot ratify this opinion, which puts the "Big Week" on the same level as July 3 and 4, 1863, days that saw Robert E. Lee and the cause of the Confederacy falling back finally before the superiority of the Union. Flying 3,000 sorties, the Americans suffered the loss of 244 bombers and 33 fighters while the R.A.F. lost 157 four-engined aircraft. The communiqué from London which announced, when the operations had finished, that 692 enemy aircraft had been shot down or destroyed on the ground, was very much mistaken in its figures.

Moreover, in spite of the carpet of bombs which fell on the factories of Braunschweig, Oschersleben, Bernburg, Leipzig, Augsburg, Regensburg, Stuttgart, Fürth, Gotha, Schweinfurt, Tutow,

▽ *Destroying key German centres of communication behind the invasion sector was a vital part of the build-up phase. This is how Orléans marshalling-yard looked after massive Allied air attacks.*

and Posen, German industry continued to build aircraft. By August 1, 1944, the average monthly figure for the first seven months of the year had reached 3,650, of which 2,500 were day fighters, 250 night fighters, and 250 bombers. All the same, Göring had to defend the vital targets, and to do this he was forced to make painful decisions and to take aircraft away from the fighter squadrons behind the Atlantic Wall. Here it is true to say that the American attack on the German aircraft industry helped the Allied landings in France.

For 36 days and 55 nights, from January 1 to June 5, 1944, the great cities of the Reich suffered 102 serious attacks which devastated Berlin (17 raids), Braunschweig (13 raids), Frankfurt (eight raids), Hanover (five raids), Magdeburg, Leipzig, Duisburg, and many others. In January, the 15th Air Force bombed Klagenfurt; on March 17, Vienna was raided for the first time. May 18 saw the port of Gdynia and the East Prussian city of Marienburg under attack. As can be seen, it was the whole of Germany which was now within range of British and American bombing aircraft.

The right targets

Though General Spaatz's success in the battle against Germany's aircraft industry had only been partial, he unquestionably won a great victory in the attack he launched at the beginning of April 1944 against the Reich's sources of liquid, natural, and synthetic fuel.

On August 1, 1943, 179 B-24 Liberators of the American 9th Air Force had taken off from Benghazi and bombed the oil-wells and installations at Ploieşti. But the success of the raid had not been equal to its boldness, for the Americans had lost 53 aircraft, eight of which were interned in Turkey. On April 4, 1944, the 15th Air Force, based around Foggia, made a fresh start with 230 four-engined bombers and produced far better results. The bombers extended their raids to refineries in Bucharest, Giurgiu, Budapest, and Vienna, to the Danube ports and the convoys of barges going up the river, and this managed to reduce the amount of oil that Germany was drawing from Rumania by 80 per cent. From 200,000 tons in February 1944, the amount had fallen to 40,000 in June.

But the most important aspect was the plan approved on April 19 by General Eisenhower, by which the 8th Air Force and Bomber Command began a systematic attack on the German synthetic fuel industry. On May 12, 935 American bombers dropped a hail of high-explosive and incendiary bombs on factories at Leuna, Böhlen, Zeitz, Lützkendorf, and Brüx. On May 28 and May 29, 1,576 British and American four-engined bombers returned to the targets and completely laid waste the great coal hydrogenation plants of Politz in Pomerania. In their struggle against German war sinews, the British

△ *A smashed German supply-train in France. Obviously the Germans would try to prevent the Allies from building up a local superiority in the beach-head; the Allies must therefore keep the flow of German reinforcements to the utter minimum or shut it off altogether.*

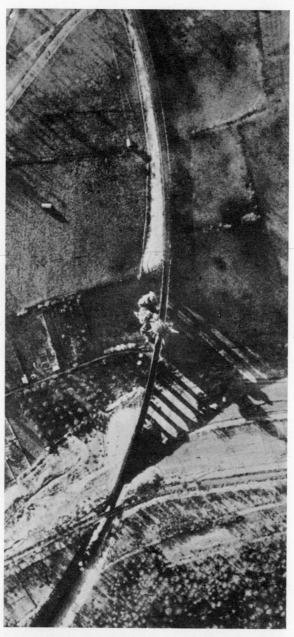

△ *B-24 Liberators unload.*
▷ *A direct hit on the viaduct at Poix. A train can be seen steaming on to the viaduct at the bottom of the picture, but subsequent air reconnaissance did not establish whether its brakes were good enough.*
▽ *Another smashed station.*

and Americans had found the right target. This was seen clearly by General Spaatz, though perhaps not by others, when on June 8 he sent a directive to the 8th and 15th Air Forces ordering them to concentrate on Germany's fuel production centres.

His views were shared by Speer, the German Minister of War Production. In a memorandum to the Führer on June 30 he wrote:

"If we cannot manage to protect our hydrogenation factories and our refineries by all possible means, it will be impossible to get them back into working order from the state they are in now. If that happens, then by September we shall no longer be capable of covering the Wehrmacht's most urgent needs. In other words, from then on there will be a gap which will be impossible to fill and which will bring in its train inevitable tragic consequences."

Albert Speer, whose organisational gifts are recognised by all, did not exaggerate matters in Hitler's style. This is clearly evident from the following table, the figures for which are taken from the book which Wolfgang Birkenfeld wrote in 1964 on the history of the manufacture of synthetic fuel during the Third Reich.

Aviation fuel (in thousands of tons)

	Programmed	Produced	Consumed
January	165	159	122
February	165	164	135
March	169	181	156
April	172	175	164

May	184	156	195
June	198	52	182
July	207	35	136
August	213	17	115
September	221	10	60
October	228	20	53
November	230	49	53
December	223	26	44

Similar conclusions could be reached from the figures for ordinary petrol and diesel fuel. It is calculated that a Panzer division, according to its 1944 establishment, consumed in battle some 55,000 gallons of fuel a day. Towards the end of summer 1944, the aircraft and tanks of the Third Reich were running on almost empty fuel tanks.

Occupied areas to be bombed?

Sir Trafford Leigh-Mallory's air forces had the mission of preparing for the landings and creating conditions which would permit the British and American armies fighting in Normandy to win the great air and ground battle over the Reich which, it was expected, would lead to final victory.

Even so, all General Eisenhower's energy and power of argument was required to get the green light from Churchill for the bombing planned, for the Prime Minister hated the idea of bombing the peoples whom Operation "Overlord" was to free from the German yoke.

According to Georg W. Feuchter, the German historian of the war in the air, S.H.A.E.F. had drawn up this timetable of objectives to be hit in the occupied countries:

"*January:* Aircraft motor and accessory factories; communications (especially the railway networks); V-1 pads; aerodromes;
February: V-1 pads; aerodromes; communications (railway networks);
March: Communications (priority still for the railways); aircraft industry (motors and accessories); V-1 pads; coastal fortifications; aerodromes;
April: Communications (railway network, with intensity increased towards the end of the month); aerodromes; V-1 pads; coastal fortifications; shipping; and
May: Concentration of attention on communications, not only fixed railway installations, but trains and road bridges; radar on the coast; V-1 pads; coastal fortifications."

Bombing objectives

1. To halt the movement of reserves
The systematic attack on communications was aimed at preventing O.K.W. and Army Group "B" reserves from reaching the battlefields. But at the same time it was at all costs essential to avoid revealing, by the choice of targets, the primary objectives of Operation "Overlord".

Bearing in mind these two contradictory requirements, which had to be satisfied at the same time, the Allied squadrons began by dropping two curtains of bombs, one along the Seine between Rouen and Paris and the other following the line of the Albert Canal from Antwerp to Liège, finishing at Namur. Within these lines, about 20 principal railway junctions were completely wiped out. As the Allies did not wish to inflict this treatment on Paris, they restricted themselves to destroying the marshalling yards of its outer suburban area: Trappes, Juvisy, and Villeneuve Saint Georges. In this way the Allies counted on preventing the German 15th Army from intervening on the left bank of the Seine and at the same time convincing German high command that the probable landing-zone was the Pas-de-Calais.

2. To cut lines of communication
Even so, Rundstedt had to be prevented from reinforcing the Normandy battlefields with the eight divisions he had in Brittany, or from Army Group "G" (Colonel-General Blaskowitz), which had 15, including three Panzer, divisions between Nantes and Hendaye and between Perpignan and Menton. This was the reason for the hail of bombs which fell at intervals on Rennes, Nantes, Le Mans, Angers, and the most important towns of the Loire valley, while the bombing of Lyons, Saint Etienne, Avignon, Marseilles, and Toulon made Hitler think an attack on the Côte d'Azur was being prepared. Finally, in Lorraine, Alsace, and Champagne, the lines along which O.K.W. might route its reserves to reinforce the Western Front were also cut.

On May 4, the bridge at Gaillon collapsed under the very eyes of Rommel, who had just completed an inspection at Riva Bella. Mantes bridge had also been

△ A stick of "heavies" makes for its target.

▽ A German housewife, clutching hastily-snatched belongings, runs from her burning home.

destroyed on the same day, leaving no other passable bridges over the Seine below Paris. On the same day the Loire bridges downstream from Blois had met the same fate.

This campaign against the railway communications of Western Europe met with absolute success, particularly because from May 1 onward the British and American tactical air forces harried locomotives, both on the track and in the repair sheds. So intense and accurate was this offensive that by June 6, railway traffic had fallen to half its January 1943 level in the rest of France and to only 13 per cent in the area north of the Loire. Catastrophic consequences for German strategy followed. Here the example often given is that of the *Waffen*-S.S. II Panzer Corps, which had been lent to Model to re-establish the line in Eastern Galicia. When the invasion was reported, the corps was entrained at L'vov and took five days to reach Nancy. After here, the railways were in such a state that the corps had to be detrained and sent to the Normandy front by road. At a time when every hour was vital, this brought it into battle four days later than calculated.

Another result of the bombing had not been foreseen by S.H.A.E.F. Because of the destruction and the absolute priority given to military transport, iron ore ceased to flow into the Saar factories, while the coal stocks at the pit-heads mounted up.

3. To destroy coastal radar and guns
Another success for British and American air forces was the action they took against the radar network set up by the Germans between Cape Gris-Nez and Cape Barfleur. Also the attack on the coastal batteries placed or in course of emplacement between Le Havre and Cherbourg brought about the destruction of a certain number of large-calibre guns or caused the Germans to move them back inland, with the result that they took no part in repelling the landings. In any case, there had been so much delay in building the concrete shelters intended to house them that they were not usable.

As for Sperrle's air force, it had been defeated in the air or wiped out on the ground and had ceased to exist. And so, as they instructed raw recruits moving up to the front, the old soldiers of the Wehrmacht would say: "If you see a white plane, it's an American; if it's black, it's the R.A.F. If you don't see any planes, it's the Luftwaffe."

△ *The spectre that hung over "Fortress Europe"—Boeing B-17's in mass formation.*
▷ *Bitter German propaganda stressing the inevitable by-product of strategic bombing: civilian deaths and maimings.*

CHAPTER 117
Assault and lodgement

Previous page: *Scottish troops of the 2nd Army wade ashore from their landing craft on June 6. Note the tanks on the beach, providing immediate support for the infantry against the shoreline strongpoints.*
△ *The Allied press celebrates the long-awaited event.*

Cornelius Ryan, in his book *The Longest Day,* emphasises the importance of the H-hour decision when he described the historic scene:

"Eisenhower now polled his commanders one by one. General Smith thought that the attack should go in on the sixth – it was a gamble, but one that should be taken. Tedder and Leigh-Mallory were both fearful that even the predicted cloud cover would prove too much for the air forces to operate effectively . . . Montgomery stuck to the decision that he had made the night before when the June 5 D-Day had been postponed. 'I would say Go,' he said.

"It was now up to Ike. The moment had come when only he could make the decision. There was a long silence as Eisenhower weighed all the possibilities. General Smith, watching, was struck by the 'isolation and loneliness' of the Supreme Commander as he sat, hands clasped before him, looking down at the table. The minutes ticked by; some say two minutes passed, others as many as five. Then Eisenhower, his face strained, looked up and announced his decision. Slowly he said, 'I am quite positive we must give the order . . . I don't like it, but there it is . . . I don't see how we can do anything else,' Eisenhower stood up. He looked tired, but some of the tension had left his face."

When one reviews the first 24 hours of Operation "Overlord", the rôle of the Resistance must first be mentioned. It was in fact vital. This opinion is based on the evidence of the Allied and German combatants, and the works on the Resistance by Colonel Rémy, Pierre Nord, and George Martelli should also be carefully considered. No military operation was ever based on such comprehensive Intelligence as "Overlord". Evidence for this is offered by the remarks of the operations officer of the 12th *"Hitlerjugend"* S.S. Panzer Division when he examined a map which had been found on June 8 in the wreck of a Canadian tank. "We were astounded at the accuracy with which all the German fortifications were marked in; even the weapons, right down to the light machine guns and mortars, were listed. And we were disgusted that our own Intelligence had not been able to stop this sort of spying. We found out, later on, that a Frenchman had been arrested who admitted that he had spied for years in the Orne sector, appearing every day in his greengrocer's van on the coastal road. We could clearly see on this map the result of his activities, and that of other spies also."

These were the results obtained by the networks organised by Colonel Rémy from 1942 onwards. Admittedly there were some slight errors and omissions in their summaries: these were inevitable. The English would probably not have embarked on the dangerous airborne attack on the Merville battery if they had known that instead of the 4-inch guns it was thought to have had, it had four 3-inch guns which were not powerful enough to affect the landing of the British 3rd Division at Riva-Bella. Similarly, the Rangers would not have scaled Pointe de Hoe had they known that its casemates were without the six long range guns they were reported to have.

General Bradley moreover did not know that Rommel had advanced five battalions from the 352nd Division to support the regiment on the left wing of the 716th Division. The two carrier-pigeons bringing news of this considerable reinforcement of the enemy's defences had been shot down in flight. However, the Allies' otherwise excellent information concerning the German army's plans was gained at the expense of considerable personal sacrifice and much loss of life.

Weather conditions against the Allies

It is well known that weather conditions played an important part in the way that the Germans were taken by surprise at dawn on June 6. They had a paralysing effect. Rommel's opinion, that the landing would only take place when dawn and high tide coincided, was also mistaken. His naval commander, Vice-Admiral Ruge, noted in his diary on June 4: "Rain and a very strong west wind". Moreover, before leaving la Roche-Guyon via Herrlingen for Berchtesgaden, Rommel noted in the Army Group "B" diary at 0600 hours on the same day that "he had no doubts about leaving as the tides would be very unfavourable for a landing in his absence,

and air reconnaissance gave no reason to think that a landing could possibly be imminent." At the same time, on the other side of the Channel, Eisenhower had just postponed "Overlord". On the next day, owing to the temporary spell of good weather forecast by Group-Captain Stagg, Eisenhower decided to cross on June 6, while the German weathermen at O.B.W. still maintained that a landing was out of the question.

Up to now the weather conditions had favoured the Allies. After midnight on June 5, the weather turned against them;

▽ *The Allies present the world's account at Germany's Atlantic Wall.*

The American/British Sherman Duplex Drive tank

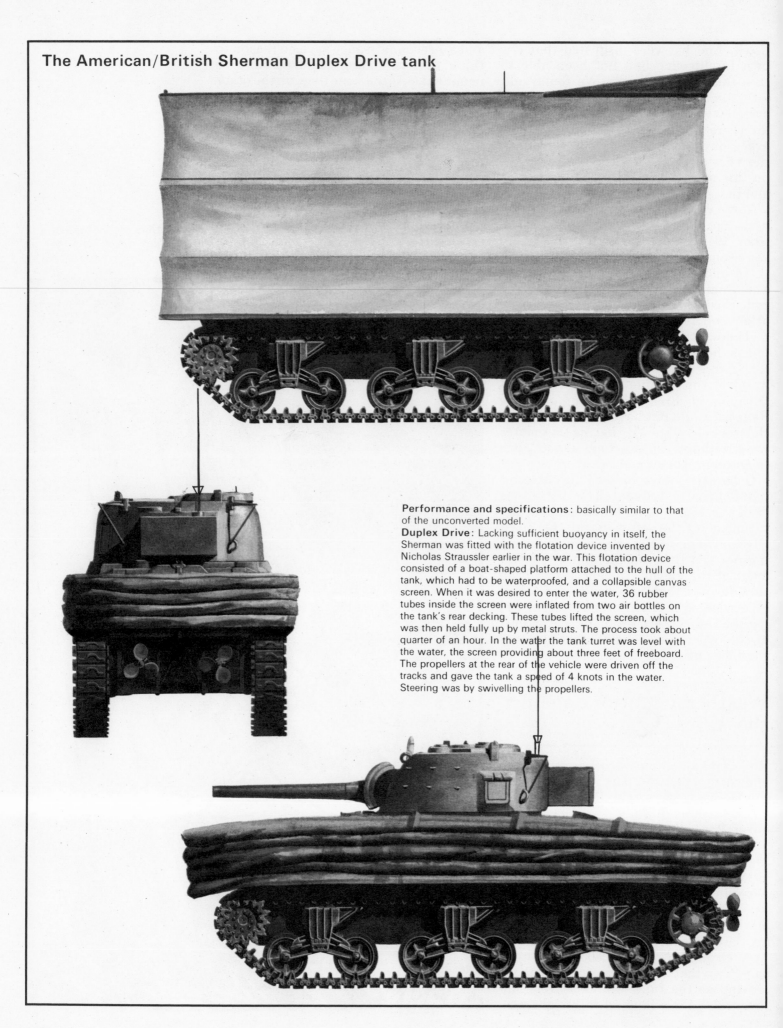

Performance and specifications: basically similar to that of the unconverted model.

Duplex Drive: Lacking sufficient buoyancy in itself, the Sherman was fitted with the flotation device invented by Nicholas Straussler earlier in the war. This flotation device consisted of a boat-shaped platform attached to the hull of the tank, which had to be waterproofed, and a collapsible canvas screen. When it was desired to enter the water, 36 rubber tubes inside the screen were inflated from two air bottles on the tank's rear decking. These tubes lifted the screen, which was then held fully up by metal struts. The process took about quarter of an hour. In the water the tank turret was level with the water, the screen providing about three feet of freeboard. The propellers at the rear of the vehicle were driven off the tracks and gave the tank a speed of 4 knots in the water. Steering was by swivelling the propellers.

although the wind had fallen a little, as Group-Captain Stagg had predicted, it was blowing strongly enough to scatter widely the paratroopers of the 82nd and 101st American Airborne Divisions, who had dropped over the Cotentin peninsula, and the British 6th Airborne Division which had dropped between the Orne and the Dives.

A few hours later, the bomber attack failed for the same reason to neutralise the "Omaha" Beach defences. In the same sector, disaster met the amphibious tank formation which was to support the left wing of the American 1st Division: of the 32 tanks which were launched into the water 8,000 yards from the shore, 27 sank like stones with most of their crews; the canvas flotation skirt supported by a tubular framework gave the tanks only about 3 feet free-board – but the sea was running with a swell of more than 3 feet. The Americans who landed between Vierville and Saint Laurent were therefore put to a gruelling test.

One other apparently accidental factor this time favoured the attackers. On the evening of June 5 Lieutenant-Colonel Hellmuth Meyer, chief Intelligence officer of the German 15th Army, interrupted Colonel-General von Salmuth's game of bridge and told him that the B.B.C. had just broadcast a special message for the French resistance networks:

"Blessent mon coeur
D'une langueur
Monotone"
(a quotation from Verlaine's poem *Chanson d'automne*).

The *Abwehr* had found out, though it is not yet known how, that the code message meant that the landing would take place within 48 hours after midnight of the day of the message.

When he received this news, the commander of the 15th Army not only alerted his staff without delay, but also transmitted this vital information to his superiors at Army Group "B", O.B.W., and O.K.W. At la Roche-Guyon Lieutenant-General Speidel, who was deputising in Rommel's absence, did not think of urging the 7th Army at Le Mans to prepare for action, and at St. Germain-en-Laye no one checked that he had done so.

In his book, *Invasion – They're Coming*, Paul Carell comments:

"Here is the well-nigh incredible story of why, nevertheless, they were caught unawares." Can we do better than the author of *Invasion – They're Coming*? Field-Marshal von Rundstedt can be exonerated, since he had just signed an Intelligence report for the German High Command. The following excerpts are taken from Cornelius Ryan's book:

"The systematic and distinct increase

△ *Men and vehicles of the U.S. 1st Army land on the coast of Normandy. The Americans, putting their amphibious tanks into the water further out than the British, suffered fairly heavy losses when the swell proved too much for the D.D. tanks and sank several.*

1629

The British Churchill Carpet-Layer Type D Mark III armoured vehicle

This was a converted Churchill designed to unroll a length of 9 feet 11 inches-wide matting over soft ground and barbed wire to facilitate the advance of other armoured vehicles, soft-skinned vehicles, and troops. The matting was carried on the "bobbin" and unrolled under the tank. When the full length of matting had been used, the "bobbin" could be jettisoned with a small explosive charge. Laying speed was 2 mph. The vehicle illustrated is fitted with deep wading gear.

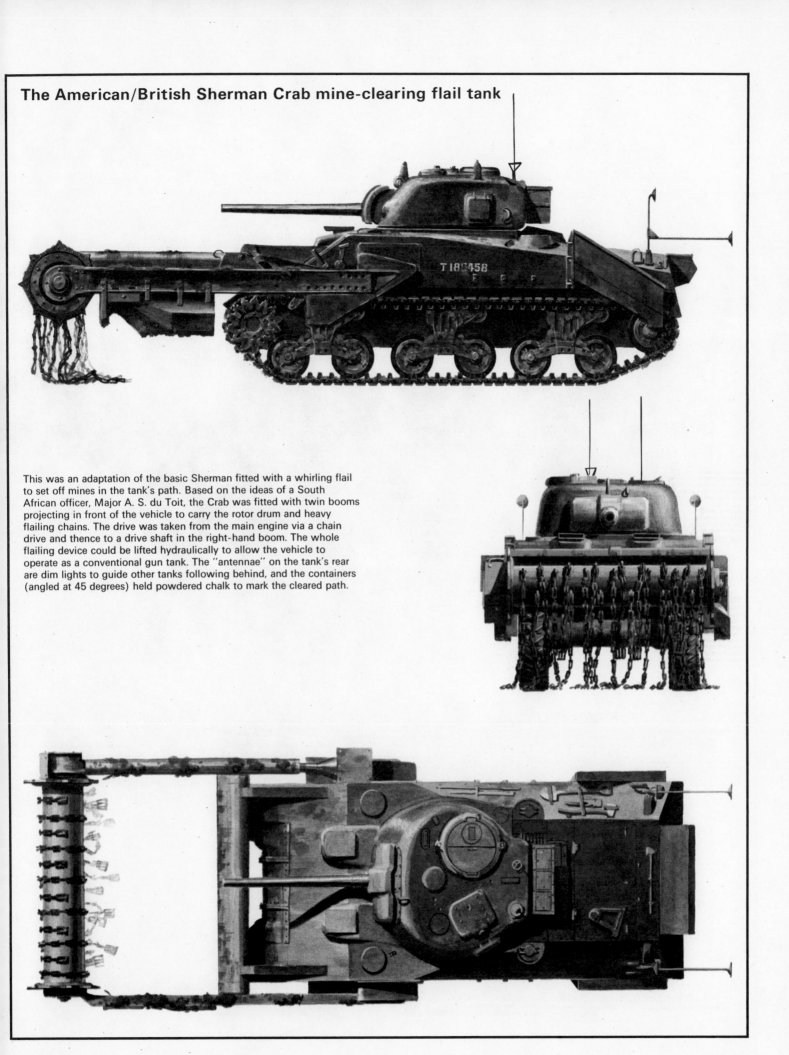

The American/British Sherman Crab mine-clearing flail tank

This was an adaptation of the basic Sherman fitted with a whirling flail to set off mines in the tank's path. Based on the ideas of a South African officer, Major A. S. du Toit, the Crab was fitted with twin booms projecting in front of the vehicle to carry the rotor drum and heavy flailing chains. The drive was taken from the main engine via a chain drive and thence to a drive shaft in the right-hand boom. The whole flailing device could be lifted hydraulically to allow the vehicle to operate as a conventional gun tank. The "antennae" on the tank's rear are dim lights to guide other tanks following behind, and the containers (angled at 45 degrees) held powdered chalk to mark the cleared path.

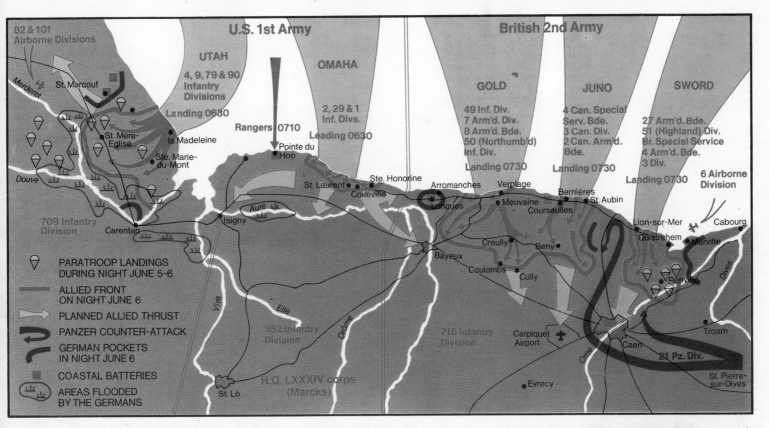

U.S. 1st Army

British 2nd Army

82 & 101
Airborne Divisions

UTAH

4, 9, 79 & 90
Infantry
Divisions

Landing 0630

OMAHA

2, 29 & 1
Inf. Divs.

Leading 0630

Rangers 0710

GOLD

49 Inf. Div.
7 Arm'd. Div.
8 Arm'd. Bde.
50 (Northumb'd)
Inf. Div.

Landing 0730

JUNO

4 Can. Special
Serv. Bde.
3 Can. Div.
2 Can. Arm'd.
Bde.

Landing 0730

SWORD

27 Arm'd. Bde.
51 (Highland) Div.
Br. Special Service
4 Arm'd. Bde.
3 Div.

Landing 0730

6 Airborne
Division

Merderet — St. Marcouf — St. Mère-Eglise — la Madeleine — Ste. Marie-du-Mont — Douve — Pointe du Hoo — St. Laurent — Colleville — Ste. Honorine — Arromanches — Verplage — Bernières — St. Aubin — Lion-sur-Mer — Quistreham — Cabourg — Merville — Meuvaine — Courseulles — Longues — Aure — Isigny — Carentan — Bayeux — Creully — Beny — Coulombs — Cully — Carpiquet Airport — Caen — Troarn — Evrecy — St. Pierre-sur-Dives — Ranville — Orne — Dives — 21 Pz. Div.

709 Infantry Division

352 Infantry Division

716 Infantry Division

Vire — Elle — Drôme — H.Q. LXXXIV corps (Marcks) — St. Lô

Legend:
- PARATROOP LANDINGS DURING NIGHT JUNE 5-6
- ALLIED FRONT ON NIGHT JUNE 6
- PLANNED ALLIED THRUST
- PANZER COUNTER-ATTACK
- GERMAN POCKETS IN NIGHT JUNE 6
- COASTAL BATTERIES
- AREAS FLOODED BY THE GERMANS

---

of air attacks indicates that the enemy has reached a high degree of readiness. The probable invasion front remains the sector from the Scheldt (in Holland) to Normandy . . . and it is not impossible that the north front of Brittany might be included . . . it is still not clear where the enemy will invade within this total area. Concentrated air attacks on the coast defences between Dunkirk and Dieppe may mean that the main Allied invasion effort will be made there . . . (but) imminence of invasion is not recognisable."

After accepting the report's rather vague conclusions (it was called *The Allies' Probable Intentions*), Rundstedt, it can be assumed, considered that the 15th Army's alert position, with its right on the Escaut and its left at Cabourg, was ready for any emergency.

One may also assume that Speidel, the chief-of-staff of Army Group "B", was still influenced by Rommel, who had said definitely the day before that the Allies could not possibly make the big attempt in his absence. Moreover, there is no doubt that too frequent alerts would have harmed the troops' morale and prejudiced their training, as well as interrupting the fortification work in which they were engaged.

Admittedly, if the 7th Army and LXXXIV Corps had been alerted at about 2300 hours on July 5, the *coup* attempted by a glider detachment of the British 6th Airborne Division and the U.S. 82nd Airborne Division's attack on Sainte Mère-Eglise would almost certainly have failed.

Allied air supremacy all important

Admiral Sir Bertram Ramsay, the commander of the naval Operation "Fortune" supporting "Overlord", is said to have likened the invasion army to a shell fired by the navy, but Montgomery asserted that only air supremacy would ensure naval supremacy.

On June 6, 1944, the Anglo-American forces conformed to the two conditions laid down by the two British war leaders. In the air General Eisenhower, faced with 419 Luftwaffe planes, had more than 10,500 fighting planes at his disposal:

    3,467 four-engined bombers
    1,645 twin-engined bombers
    5,409 fighter bombers and interceptor fighters

Therefore he was in a position to use 2,355 transport planes and 867 gliders carrying about 27,000 troops and their *matériel* including light tanks, with no risk of attack by German fighters, though there was still the threat of anti-aircraft defences.

◁ *American infantry come ashore.*
△ *Hitler's fond dream that the Allies' "European adventure" would be "fatal". It could have been, but for Hitler's foolish insistence that the landings in Normandy were only a feint.*

△ Part of the vast Allied invasion force wallows in the Channel off Normandy, unhindered by the weather and virtually undisturbed by the Luftwaffe.

▽ Men of the 3rd Canadian Division disembark at Courselles, on "Juno" Beach.

The Allied invasion fleet

At sea, the embarkation fleet from British ports consisted of 4,126 transport vessels, including converted liners acting as floating headquarters to the major units being landed, and the LCT(R) support craft firing salvoes of 792 5-inch rockets which saturated an area of 750 by 160 yards. This fleet included 1,173 large and small ships transporting armoured vehicles, which shows how important it was for the infantry attacking the Atlantic Wall to have support from tanks and their guns. The fleet for the initial assault consisted (it is reliably reported) of 1,213 ships of all sizes flying seven different flags; three-quarters of them flew the Royal Navy's White Ensign. They included:

7 battleships (3 American)
2 monitors
23 cruisers (3 American, 2 French, 1 Polish)
80 destroyers (34 American, 2 Polish, 2 Norwegian)
25 torpedo-boats (1 French, 2 Polish, 1 Norwegian)
63 corvettes (3 French, 2 Norwegian, 2 Greek)
2 Dutch gunboats
98 minesweepers (9 American)

Of this fleet, all the warships, monitors and gunboats, 18 cruisers and about 50 destroyers had been assigned fire targets of the German batteries between Villerville (opposite Le Havre) and the Barfleur cape: these batteries were therefore engaged by 52 12-inch, 14-inch, and 15-

inch guns and more than 500 medium calibre guns whose fire was all the more effective as it was controlled from the air by Spitfire fighters especially detailed for this purpose.

This huge fleet of 5,339 ships was in the Channel on Sunday June 4 when it received the signal that the assault was deferred from the following day to June 6; a part of the fleet spent the day cruising in the area. But the bad weather which caused the postponement also kept the Luftwaffe patrols grounded; otherwise they would have spotted and reported this unusual concentration of ships. On the evening of June 5 the fleet assembled south of the Isle of Wight and made for its objectives in ten columns.

Admiral Lemonnier, who was on the bridge of the *Montcalm,* described the night crossing: "Spotted the buoy at the entrance to the channel which we must follow for four hours behind a flotilla of minesweepers.

"Now we are only doing 6 knots. The sweepers aren't moving. Possibly they've found some mines and the rough sea is hampering them in their work.

"We have to stop continually. We can only move forward in fits, as we have to take care to stay in our narrow channel. This isn't the time to be put stupidly out of action by a mine.

"We feel as though we are in one of those endless rows of cars blocked outside a big city on a Sunday evening, moving forward by pressing the accelerator slightly, then putting the brake on, touching the rear light of the car ahead – with one difference, that here there is not the slightest light to mark the stern of the ship ahead. Luckily there is just enough light to make out the outlines of the *Georges Leygues* and to keep a look-out."

△ *Men of the Commandos start on their dangerous trek to the dubious shelter of the shore through heavy German machine gun and mortar fire.*

Ramsay's objectives

Admiral Ramsay had divided his forces into two:
1. Under the American Rear-Admiral A. G. Kirk, the Western Naval Task Force was to land and support the American V and VII Corps on the "Utah" and "Omaha" Beaches on both sides of the Vire estuary. All ships flying the Stars and Stripes, including the *Nevada,* a survivor from Pearl Harbor, had appropriately been assigned to him.
2. Under Rear-Admiral Sir Philip Vian,

◁ ◁ *The build-up starts. As the front line troops pressed inland, the beach-heads were consolidated and prepared for the follow-up divisions and the* matériel *that would be needed for the breakout into France proper.*
◁ *First to land were the airborne troops. Seen here are men of the British 6th Airborne Division, which was to land on and hold the left flank of the 2nd Army's sector until the conventional ground forces reached them.*

the Eastern Naval Task Force was to perform identical services for the British I and XXX Corps which were to come ashore between Ver-Plage and Ouistreham on the beaches called (from west to east), "Gold", "Juno", and "Sword".

When reviewing the Allied air and naval forces, the power and quality of the support they gave the land forces in the hard fighting against the defenders of the Atlantic Wall must be emphasised. For example, two of the three Czechoslovak 8-inch guns comprising the Saint Marcouf battery had been destroyed; similarly the four 6-inch guns of the Longues battery, near Port-en-Bessin, were silenced by the fire of the cruisers *Ajax, Montcalm,* and *Georges Leygues.* In addition, the Allied forces over the battle sector had been increased and they responded rapidly, accurately and efficiently to all requests from the ground forces. From dawn to dusk they had made over 4,600 sorties, while only about 50 planes reminded both sides of the Luftwaffe's existence.

The Germans guarding the coast on the night of June 5-6 were frequently caught off their guard, and several comic incidents were reported. Paul Carell gives an example:

"Hoffman stepped outside the bunker. He gave a start. Six giant birds were making straight for his battle head-quarters. They were clearly visible, for

the moon had just broken through the clouds. 'They're bailing out.' For an instant Hoffman thought the aircraft had been damaged and its crew was going to jump. But then he understood. This was an airborne landing by para-troops. The white mushrooms were float-ing down–straight at his bunker.

"'Alarm! Enemy parachutists!' The men at 3rd Battalion head-quarters had never pulled on their trousers so fast before.

"Besides reports of parachute landings, radar stations began to signal huge concentrations of aircraft.

"But both in Paris and in Rastenburg the news was received sceptically. 'What,

△ *Safe landing for a British Horsa glider beside a tree-lined road.*
Overleaf: *The American landings.*

in this weather?' Even the chief-of-staff C.-in-C. West scoffed: 'Maybe a flock of seagulls?'"

At the end of the first day, Eisenhower and Montgomery were in a position to make the following estimate of their gains and losses:

On the whole, the landing had been successful, but the Americans and the British had nowhere gained their prescribed objectives for the evening of D-Day. North of the Vire the American 82nd and 101st Airborne Divisions, under Major-Generals M. B. Ridgway and M. D. Taylor respectively, which were due to protect VII Corps' right (Lieutenant-General J. L. Collins) and give it access to the right bank of the Merderet, had scattered in small pockets in the night; in addition they lost many men and much

had been completely and devastatingly effective.

"In Ste. Mère-Eglise, as the stunned townspeople watched from behind their shuttered windows, paratroops of the 82nd's 505th Regiment slipped cautiously through the empty streets. The church bell was silent now. On the steeple Private John Steele's empty parachute hung limp . . .

"Passing round the back of the church, P. F. C. William Tucker reached the square and set up his machine-gun behind a tree. Then as he looked out on the moonlit square he saw a parachute and, lying next to him, a dead German. On the far side were the crumpled, sprawled shapes of other bodies. As Tucker sat there in the semi-darkness trying to figure out what happened, he began to feel that

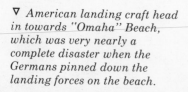

▽ *American landing craft head in towards "Omaha" Beach, which was very nearly a complete disaster when the Germans pinned down the landing forces on the beach.*

matériel in the shallow floods and minefields laid by the Germans. In short, of the 17,262 fighting men of the two divisions who jumped or landed on "the longest day", 2,499, or nearly 15 per cent, were missing.

Nevertheless a regiment from the 82nd Airborne Division had occupied the small town of Sainte Mère-Eglise (because of the panic flight of a service unit of German A.A. defences), maintained its ground, and in the evening had made contact with the American 4th Division which had landed on "Utah" Beach. This unit under Major-General Barton had had a relatively easy task, as the air and naval bombardment on the support points of the German 709th Division (Lieutenant-General von Schlieben) barring its way

he was not alone—that somebody was standing behind him. Grabbing the cumbersome machine-gun, he whirled around. His eyes came level with a pair of boots slowly swaying back and forth. Tucker hastily stepped back. A dead paratrooper was hanging in the tree looking down at him.

"Then (Lt.-Colonel) Krause pulled an American flag from his pocket. It was old and worn—the same flag that the 505th had raised over Naples . . . He walked to the townhall, and on the flagpole by the side of the door, ran up the colours. There was no ceremony. In the square of the dead paratroopers the fighting was over. The Stars and Stripes flew over the first town to be liberated by the Americans in France."

Power of the Allied offensive

Paul Carell, who conducted a careful survey among the German survivors of this campaign, describes the destruction of the defence-works W.5 surrounding the beach near the small village of la Madeleine.

"All the fortifications they had laboriously dug and built through the weeks had been churned up like a children's sand-pit. The 75-millimetre anti-tank gun was a heap of twisted metal. The 88-millimetre gun had taken some bad knocks. Two ammunition bunkers had blown up. The machine-gun nests had

been buried by avalanches of sand.

"Immediately the infernal concert started – rockets. They were firing only at the two corner bunkers with their 50-millimetre armoured carrier-cannon. The rockets slammed against the bunkers. They smacked through the apertures. The left bunker blew up at once, evidently a direct hit, through the aperture, among the stored shells. The bunker on the right was enveloped in smoke and flames. When the attack was over both bunkers and guns were only rubble and scrap metal. The crews had been killed or severely wounded."

A plane appeared and disappeared. "But evidently it delivered its message. The heavy naval bombardment began. Continuous, uninterrupted hell. Blow upon

blow the huge shells crashed into the strongpoint. Trenches were levelled. Barbed wire was torn to shreds. Minefields were blown up. Bunkers were drowned in the loose sand of the dunes. The stone building with the telephone exchange crumbled. The fire-control posts of the flame-throwers received a direct hit."

It is not therefore surprising that the losses of the American 4th Division amounted only to 197 killed, wounded, and missing on June 6. At midnight the whole division had landed (with the exception of one battery), a total of 21,328 men, 1,742 vehicles, and 1,950 tons of *matériel*, munitions, and fuel.

When it landed at "Omaha", the American 1st Division (Major-General C. R. Huebner) had been given the main road N.

△ △ *Commandos press inland from the beach area. Note the "funny" bridging tank in the background.*
△ *The beach area. Only by the most careful planning and training were the schedules so vital for success ensured, and the chaos that could so easily have jeopardised the whole operation avoided.*

13, which runs from Caen to Cherbourg, as its objective for the day. This required an advance of three miles from the Vierville beach. It was also to extend its right as far as Isigny and its left as far as the western approach to Bayeux, where it was to make contact with the inner flank of the British 2nd Army. For this purpose Major-General L. T. Gerow, commander of V Corps, had reinforced his corps with a combined regiment drawn from the 29th Division. At nightfall the 1st Division had not got beyond the small villages of Saint Laurent and Colleville.

In addition the air bombardment had missed its target, the majority of the D.D. tanks had sunk before they reached the beaches, and the 1st Division had come up against eight battalions, though they had expected to meet and destroy three. The Germans moreover had held their fire as long as possible. At about 1000 hours General Bradley, the commander of the American 1st Army, had sent ashore his chief-of-staff and received a discouraging report from him:

"The 1st Division lay pinned down behind the sea wall while the enemy swept the beaches with small-arms fire. Artillery chased the landing craft where they milled offshore. Much of the difficulty had been caused by the under-water obstructions. Not only had the demolition teams suffered paralysing casualties, but much of their equipment had been swept away. Only six paths had been blown in that barricade before the tide halted their operations. Unable to break through the obstacles that blocked their assigned beaches, craft turned toward Easy Red where the gaps had been blown. Then as successive waves ran in toward the cluttered beach-head they soon found themselves snarled in a jam offshore."

Admiral Kirk, however, had no intention of letting his colleagues on land bleed to death; he bunched together his destroyers on the coast, and they fired at the maximum rate on all the German fire-points that showed themselves. At the same time, the German 352nd Division battery positions began running out of shells, and as the Allies' cruisers and their tactical air forces attacked all the cross-roads, the Germans were not able to supply their artillery with fresh ammunition. At about 1300 hours, the crisis was over and the infantrymen, after the sappers had blown up the anti-tank dike

surrounding the beach, infiltrated the German position through the narrow gullies running up the cliff.

During the night of June 6-7, the remainder of the 29th Division (Major-General C. H. Gerhardt) was landed. But V Corps' losses had been heavy: 3,881 killed, wounded, and missing.

New breaches in Atlantic Wall

The British 2nd Army (General Miles C. Dempsey) had been assigned Bayeux, Caen, and Troarn (9 miles east of Caen) as its D-Day objectives. It was also

◁ *Naval gunfire support: the British cruiser* Orion *unlooses at a German coastal battery. Building on the experience gained in landings along the Italian coast, the Allied naval task forces provided very effective support for the land forces in the beach-head areas.*
◁▽ *The invasion fleet, as seen from one of the most powerful of the escorts and support ships, the battleship* Warspite.
◁▽▽ *American troops inspect the results of gunfire support: an 11-inch gun casemate comprehensively destroyed by heavy shells.*
▽ *One of the American beach-heads. Note the emergency breakwater formed by the row of ships parallel to the shore.*

ordered to extend its reconnaissance to Villers-Bocage and Evrecy, that is along approximately 18 miles of the Calvados coast. This ambitious programme was not fulfilled.

The British 6th Airborne Division (Major-General Richard N. Gale) was to protect the flanks of the operation. It was ordered:

1. To capture intact the bridges across the Orne and its canal between Bénouville and Ranville;
2. To destroy the Merville battery;
3. To destroy the Dives bridges between Troarn and the coast.

Although the wind prevented the paratroopers from landing accurately on their targets, the division completed these three missions brilliantly. At 0030 hours the British sappers and infantry had jumped from five gliders and captured the Bénouville bridges, clearing them of mines. At about 0400 hours Lieutenant-Colonel Otway had only collected 150 paratroopers from his battalion which was practically without *matériel,* and the gliders which were due to land on the superstructure of the defence works had failed to appear. Nevertheless, he had captured the Merville battery in a fierce fight in which he lost 70 dead and wounded, whilst the garrison of 130 men was left with only 22 survivors. The Dives mission was also completely successful. "All around the battery", according to Georges Blond, "the grass was strewn with corpses, British and German mixed together. Several attackers who had already gone into the defence works ran back:

" 'The guns aren't 6-inch, sir, they're 3-inch.'

" 'Fine,' said Otway, 'Blow them up.'

"The British had lost 5 officers and 65 N.C.O.'s and men, killed and wounded in the attack. It was now nearly dawn. Otway saw one of his officers apparently searching for something in his battle-dress blouse:

" 'What are you doing?'

" 'I'm sending a message to England, sir.'

"The communications officer pulled a pigeon with closed wings from his breast, turning its little head from side to side. It had taken part in the attack too. When it was released, it rose unhesitatingly into the whitening sky."

At dawn, Rear-Admiral Vian's naval forces opened fire on the German defences, and up to nightfall discharged 500 15-inch shells, 3,500 6-inch shells, and 1,380 small calibre missiles. They made

◁ *Part of the non-stop flood of men, vehicles, and* matériel *that poured ashore after the beach-head had been consolidated.*

◁▽ *Metal matting to help vehicles across the soft sand at the water's edge.*

▽ *American reinforcements disembark from a landing craft and remuster before moving up towards the front.*

wide breaches in the Atlantic Wall. Two further circumstances favoured the British landing. First, the amphibious tanks were lowered into the water much closer to the shore than at "Omaha", and were sometimes landed directly on the beaches. Secondly, large numbers of the special vehicles designed by Major-General Sir Percy Hobart, commander of the 79th Armoured Division, were used in the first waves of the infantry attack.

In addition to the Crabs, or flail tanks, which cleared the ground of the mines obstructing their tracks and had been used since El Alamein, the British 2nd Army also brought its Crocodiles and its A.V.R.E.s into the line: the Crocodiles were flame-thrower tanks which cast a 360-foot jet of burning oil beyond the range of the enemy's rocket-launchers; these tanks had trailers filled with about 400 gallons of fuel and could sustain prolonged actions; the A.V.R.E.s were mortar tanks carrying a 9-inch mortar on a Churchill tank chassis, and intended for work against armoured strongpoints.

On the other hand, against the British I and XXX Corps (commanded respectively by Lieutenant-Generals G. T. Bucknall and J. T. Crocker) the German 716th Division (Lieutenant-General W. Richter) only had four battalions and their quality

◁ U.S. infantry await the moment of truth.
△ Rudimentary mechanisation: British infantry bring their bicycles ashore.

was inferior to that of the Allies.

In these conditions, the 50th Division (Major-General D. A. H. Graham), the advance-guard of XXX Corps, proceeded from "Gold" Beach without much difficulty. By the end of the day it had some armour at the approaches of Bayeux and had moved forward about six miles.

In I Corps, the 3rd Canadian Division (Major-General R. F. L. Keller) had a more difficult landing because the Calvados reefs presented a natural obstacle; nevertheless it had advanced eight miles from Bernières ("Juno" Beach) and was near its objective, the Carpiquet airfield. On the other hand the armoured column which it had launched towards Evrecy was driven back with losses above Bretteville-l'Orgueilleuse. The result was that between its left at Saint Aubin-sur-Mer

and the right of the 50th Division, towards Arromanches, the Atlantic Wall had been breached over a front of 12 miles.

Landing at "Sword" Beach in the Riva-Bella area, the British 3rd Division (Major-General G. T. Rennie) had managed to join with the 6th Airborne Division over the Bénouville bridge. In the evening it had advanced to Biéville three miles north of Caen and repelled a counter-attack from the 21st Panzer Division. With its right close up against Lion-sur-Mer it was four or five miles from the Canadian 3rd Division.

D-Day casualties

The British 2nd Army had a total of less than 3,000 killed, wounded, and missing on D-Day.

Allied naval and air losses were insignificant: 114 planes, mainly brought down by A.A. fire; some landing craft and two destroyers—one of these, the *Corry* (U.S. Navy) blew up on a mine in the "Utah" Beach waters; the other, the Norwegian *Svenner*, succumbed to an attack on the Eastern Naval Task Force by three German destroyers from Le Havre commanded by Lieutenant-Commander Hoffmann.

Hitler holds back reinforcements

At 0111 hours (German time) General Erich Marcks, commander of LXXXIV Corps, was at his H.Q. in Saint Lô celebrating his 53rd birthday when he heard from the 716th Division that the paratroopers were coming down between the Orne and the Dives and that the bridges of these two rivers were apparently their objectives. Twenty minutes later the 709th Division signalled the landing of American paratroopers on both sides of the Merderet in the Sainte Mère-Eglise area. Quite correctly, Marcks decided that this was the invasion. He therefore alerted the troops on the coast and informed the 7th Army H.Q. at Le Mans.

The 7th Army quickly transmitted the information to la Roche-Guyon and Saint Germain. Although he hesitated when he received LXXXIV Corps' appreciation, supported by the 7th Army,

The Germans resisted the invasion with great tenacity, but the sheer size of the landing forces alone was almost too much for them. Except where terrain made the Allies' task particularly difficult, all that the Germans could do was to try to contain the invasion. It was a hard, an impossible task.
▽ *Outside Sainte Mère-Eglise.*
▷ *In the American sector: Staff Sergeant Jack Scarborough of Bossier City, Louisiana, with a German corpse outside a captured German bunker.*

△ A Sherman Crab anti-mine flail tank moves up. The correct and widespread use of such specialised armour played a very significant part in the Allies' success.

▽ A British Sherman Duplex Drive tank advances towards a Horsa glider. Note the folded flotation screen on top of the hull.

Rundstedt alerted the Panzer-*"Lehr"* Division and the 12th *"Hitlerjugend"* Panzer Division and contacted O.K.W., but Hitler forbade him to move them till further orders, which would be given him as soon as the situation was clear.

There was no further news till 0630 hours, when information was received that the Calvados coast defences were being subjected to intensive naval bombardment. At that time, however, the Führer, who had gone to bed as usual two

hours earlier, was fast asleep, thanks to Dr. Morell's pills, and no one dared to have him woken. When they finally plucked up the courage, Hitler's reaction was fairly dramatic:

"He was in a dressing-gown when he came out of his bedroom. He listened calmly to the report of his aides and then sent for O.K.W.'s chief, Field-Marshal Wilhelm Keitel, and Jodl. By the time they arrived Hitler was dressed and waiting – and excited.

"The conference that followed was, as Pultkamer recalls, 'extremely agitated'. Information was scanty, but on the basis of what was known Hitler was convinced that this was not the main invasion, and he kept repeating that over and over again. The conference lasted only a few minutes and ended abruptly, as Jodl was later to remember, when Hitler suddenly thundered at him and Keitel, 'Well, is it or isn't it the invasion?'"

Therefore it was only at 1432 that Army Group "B" received the authority, which it had sought for 12 hours, to order the 12th S.S. Panzer Division to support the 7th Army, and at 1507 hours to move the *Waffen*-S.S. I Panzer Corps and the Panzer-*"Lehr"* Division.

But after so much delay, Colonel-General Dollmann now showed excessive haste. Lieutenant-General Bayerlein, commander of the Panzer-*"Lehr"* Division, after leaving his unit to obtain instructions from 7th Army H.Q., was ordered to move towards Caen at 1700 hours. Without success the former chief-of-staff of the *Afrika Korps* (who had had much experience of British air tactics) attempted to persuade Dollmann how foolish it was to set out on the French roads before nightfall. Nevertheless Dollmann kept to his decision, thinking he would thus be able to bring the Panzer-*"Lehr"* Division into action south of Caen at dawn on the following day, June 7. But the first bombs began falling before Bayerlein and his staff had passed Beaumont-sur-Sarthe, south of Alençon.

"For once we were lucky. But the columns were getting farther and farther apart all the time. Since the Army had ordered a radio silence we had to maintain contact by dispatch riders. As if radio silence could have stopped the fighter-bombers and reconnaissance planes from spotting us! All it did was prevent the divisional staff from forming a picture of the state of the advance–if it was moving smoothly or whether there were hold-ups and losses. I was for ever sending off officers or else seeking out units myself.

"We were moving along all five routes of advance. Naturally our move had been spotted by enemy air-reconnaissance. And before long the bombers were hovering above the roads, smashing cross-roads, villages, and towns along our line of advance, and pouncing on the long columns of vehicles. At 2300 we drove through Sées. The place was lit up by

△ *A Panther tank. Despite the Allies' considerable numerical superiority in* matériel, *the Panther was a tank still very much to be feared.*
◁ *Another of Germany's best weapons, the dreaded Nebelwerfer.*
▽ *Another of Britain's specialised armoured vehicles, the Churchill Assault Vehicle Royal Engineers (A.V.R.E.), fitted with a spigot mortar to fire a 40-lb "dustbin" demolition charge up to 230 yards.*

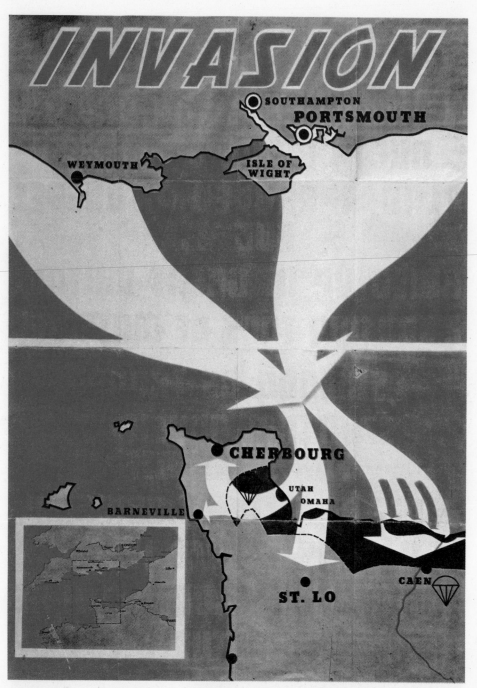

from la Roche-Guyon, he sent his armoured regiment to follow them. At 0700 hours, he was informed that he was subordinate to the 7th Army; two hours later that he would now take his orders from LXXXIV Corps.

But now General Marcks was becoming more aware of the danger from the sea; for this reason, at 1000 hours, he ordered his new subordinate to abandon the action his armoured regiment was about to take against the enemy para-troopers, and to send it over the Orne to give support to the 716th Division units barring the approach to Caen from the British. This move was completed at 1430 hours and the Germans counter-attacked at 1700 hours. At nightfall the 21st Panzer Division had managed to reach Luc-sur-Mer with its infantry, but its armoured regiment had been engaged by the British 3rd Division and had suffered heavy losses. Moreover it had nearly run out of petrol. Therefore Feuchtinger, who had 146 tanks and 51 assault guns when the engagement commenced, retreated on orders, abandoning the wrecks of 40 tracked vehicles.

The German position

At 1300 hours, a report from LXXXIV Corps to the 7th Army gave an accurate description of the fluctuations of this merciless struggle: "In the Caen area, in the British sector, the enemy is success-ful. East of the American sector, the landing is more or less repulsed at Vierville. Our counter-attack is in pro-gress in the Sainte Mère-Eglise district; the 8th Regiment of the American 4th Division (Colonel van Fleet) is pinned down there. Where is our air support? Enemy aircraft prevent us from moving or supplying our troops by day."

At midnight, an entry in the 7th Army's signals diary showed the worsening situa-tion in the afternoon in the Caen sector:

"2400 hours. 716 Infantry Division is still defending itself at strongpoints. Communications between division, regi-mental and battalion headquarters, how-ever, no longer exist, so that nothing is known as to the number of strong-points still holding out or of those liquidated ... The Chief-of-Staff of Seventh Army gives the order that the counter attack of June 7 must reach the coast without fail, since the strong-point defenders expect it of us."

△ *A simplified view of the mounting and primary objectives of Operation "Overlord".*

flares hanging above it like candles on a Christmas-tree, and heavy bombs were crashing down on the houses which were already burning. But we managed to get through."

In the Saint Pierre-sur-Dives region, the 21st Panzer Division (Major-General Feuchtinger) was in a rather different situation: it was Army Group "B"'s reserve, but its commander was author-ised to put his infantry into action to support the 716th Division if there was a landing; however, he was not allowed to engage his armour. In accordance with these orders Feuchtinger launched one of his grenadier regiments on the right bank of the Orne to engage the British paratroopers and as he received no orders

CHAPTER 118
The Panzers attack

The Battle of Normandy started very unpromisingly for the Wehrmacht. Nevertheless the Allies took a little more than six weeks to break out of the Avranches bottleneck, although according to plans they should have done so on D+20, June 27; they required another three weeks to complete the defeat of Army Group "B". This delay was due to two different factors:

1. The Normandy *bocage* (mixed woodland and pastureland), where the defenders were undoubtedly favoured by their natural surroundings. The countryside between Troarn and Bayeux, the British 2nd Army sector, was certainly suitable for use by armoured formations, but it assisted the German tanks and anti-tank devices even more; the range of their guns was greater than the Allies'. Moreover in the Norman *bocage* between Bayeux and the western Cotentin coast, the U.S. 1st Army sector, there were fields surrounded by tall, thick hedges with sunken roads between them, very suitable for ambushes, whether by the *Chouans* at the time of the French Revolution, or by the German grenadiers, who spotted enemy tanks and discharged the almost invariably lethal shots from *Panzerfaust* or *Panzerschreck* launchers at very short range. The attackers' task was also complicated by the rivers Vire, Taute, Douve, and Merderet, marshy tracts, and the 7th Army's flooding operations. General Bradley wrote: "Not even in Tunisia had we found more exasperating defensive terrain. Collins called it no less formidable than the jungles of Guadalcanal."

2. The inferior quality of their armour compared with the Germans' was another very serious handicap for the Allies. The journalist Alan Moorehead, who was a war correspondent at Montgomery's G.H.Q., stated quite frankly after the end of the war: "Our tanks were Shermans, Churchills and Cromwells. None of them was the equal of the German Mark V (the Panther), or the Mark VI (the Tiger) . . .

"The Germans had much thicker armour than we had. Their tanks were effective at a thousand yards or more: ours at ranges around five hundred yards . . . Our tanks were unequal to the job because they were not good enough. There may be various ways of dodging this plain truth, but anyone who wishes to do so will find himself arguing with the crews of more than three British armoured divisions which fought in France."

Admittedly Moorehead was a journalist, but General Bradley is recognised as one of the best brains in the American army. "Originally", he wrote, "the Sherman had come equipped with a 75-mm gun, an almost totally ineffective weapon against the heavy frontal plate of these German tanks. Only by swarming around the panzers to hit them on the flank,

▽ *The first German prisoners taken in Normandy wait in a P.O.W. cage on the beach for transportation to England.*

could our Shermans knock the enemy
out. But too often the American tankers
complained it cost them a tank or two,
with crews, to get the enemy's panzers
but only by expending more tanks than
we cared to lose. Ordance thereafter
replaced the antedated 75 with a new
76-mm high-velocity gun. But even this

new weapon often scuffed rather than
penetrated the enemy's armour.

"Eisenhower was angry when he heard
of these limitations of the new 76."

We shall not imitate him, as we know
that the Pzkw V Panther had an armour
thickness of $4\frac{1}{2}$ inches and the Pzkw VI
Tiger $5\frac{1}{2}$ inches. The British got their best
results when they re-armed their Sher-
mans with the 17-pounder anti-tank
guns which they had had since 1943.
Firing an armour-piercing shell at an
initial velocity of about 2,900 feet per
second, it was certainly superior to the
American version, but nevertheless it
was markedly inferior to the Panther's
7.5-cm, which fired at 3,068 feet per second,
and even more to the 8.8-cm of the Tiger
II or the *Königstiger* with shells of 20-
and 22-lb with a higher velocity,
which at 500 yards could penetrate 112
and 182-mm of armour respectively. Even
worse, the British and the Americans
found that their Shermans were inclined
to catch fire suddenly like bowls of
flaming punch.

However, the Panzers' undeniable tech-

◁ Undisputed master of the first tank battles in Normandy: the Tiger, with all its earlier teething troubles eliminated. In the hands of a master Panzer technician like Hauptsturmführer Wittmann, the Tiger was a deadly weapon. In a classic battle Wittmann's solitary Tiger knocked out 25 British tanks within minutes.

nical superiority was of little help to Rommel, as he was unable to supply them with the required fuel or to defend them against the continuous attacks of the Allied tactical air force, of which they were rightly a priority target.

The word *Jabo* (*Jagdbomber*: fighter-bomber) recurs in all the accounts left by the German combatants after the Normandy battle. In their attacks against enemy armour, the Allies preferred rockets, which were more accurate than bombs and more effective than the 20-mm or 40-mm shell. The R.A.F.'s Hawker Typhoon fighter carried eight 60-pounder rockets, whilst the Republic P-47 Thunderbolt had ten 5-inch anti-tank rockets.

In this ground-air battle, the rôle of the Allied engineers has perhaps not been sufficiently appreciated. They quickly cleared the rubble left in the Normandy towns and villages by the bombardments and restored communications as the troops moved forward. They also had better equipment, notably in machines of American manufacture, and in the Bailey bridge, which had prefabricated components and could be assembled in a great variety of combinations. By May 8 1945, 7,500 Bailey bridges had been built in the Western and Italian war theatres; they certainly contributed not only to the defeat of the Third Reich, but also to the

reconstruction of this part of the continent.

On June 7 and 8 successively the 12th "Hitlerjugend" S.S. Panzer Division and the Panzer-"Lehr" Division failed to drive the British back to the Channel. On June 7 the first of these major units (which under Major-General Witt included 177 tanks and 28 assault guns) should have counter-attacked in the direction of the Douvres operational base (six miles north

△ Another weapon used in Normandy: a remote-controlled tank, about the size of a Bren gun carrier, designed to deliver a heavy explosive charge into the Allied lines.

of Caen) with the 21st Panzer Division, which was immediately to its left. It managed to maul a Canadian armoured brigade in the Carpiquet region but when it reached its goal it was halted by massive artillery fire and turned to the left.

The following day the Panzer-*"Lehr"* Division came into the line on the left of the 12th S.S. Panzer Division, but between Sées and Tilly-sur-Seulles it had lost five tanks, 84 all-purpose transport vehicles, 90 cars and lorries, and 40 petrol tankers; these considerable losses caused no less concern to Lieutenant-General Bayerlein than the 12th S.S. Panzer Division's had to his colleague Witt. Moreover Vice-Admiral Ruge noted in his personal diary at the la Roche-Guyon H.Q., to which Rommel had returned late in the afternoon on June 6: "The enemy's air superiority is having the effect the Field-Marshal had foreseen: our movements are extremely slow, supplies don't get through, any deployment is becoming impossible, the artillery can't move to its firing positions any more. Precisely the same thing is happening on land here as happened at sea in the Tunisian campaign."

On June 8, when the U.S. 1st Army and the British 2nd Army joined up at Bayeux, Rundstedt put Rommel in charge of *Panzergruppe* "West", which became responsible for the conduct of operations in the sector between the mouth of the Dives and the Tilly-sur-Seulles area, while the 7th Army from now on faced the Americans alone. General Geyr von Schweppenburg, when he assumed this heavy task, was assigned the mission of retaking Bayeux and he proposed that he should break through to the Channel with his three Panzer divisions. But as soon as he set up his headquarters in the Thury–Harcourt region, he was seriously wounded in an air attack which killed many of his staff. Sepp Dietrich took over and ordered his troops to stay on the defensive while they waited for better days.

Intervention of the heavy Panzers

In fact on June 12, with the intervention of the 2nd Panzer Division (Lieutenant-General von Lüttwitz) which had been brought up from the Amiens region,

Dietrich managed to halt an attempt by the British XXX Corps which had launched the 7th Armoured Division (Major-General G. W. Erskine) against its left wing and its rear. The celebrated Desert Rats got the worst of this chance encounter, which was fought for Villers-Bocage, not for lack of energy and courage but because they were let down by their *matériel*. Chester Wilmot proves this in his description of the episode:

"The troops had dismounted to stretch their legs while the tanks reconnoitred the way ahead, when the crack of a gun split the crisp morning air and the leading half-track burst into flames. Out of the

◁ *Mobile fire-power for U.S. armoured divisions: an M7 howitzer motor carriage. The M7 carried a 105-mm howitzer and was known as the "Priest" by the British because of its pulpit-like machine gun position. It had a crew of seven.*
▽ *Canadian troops move up in the Caen sector.*

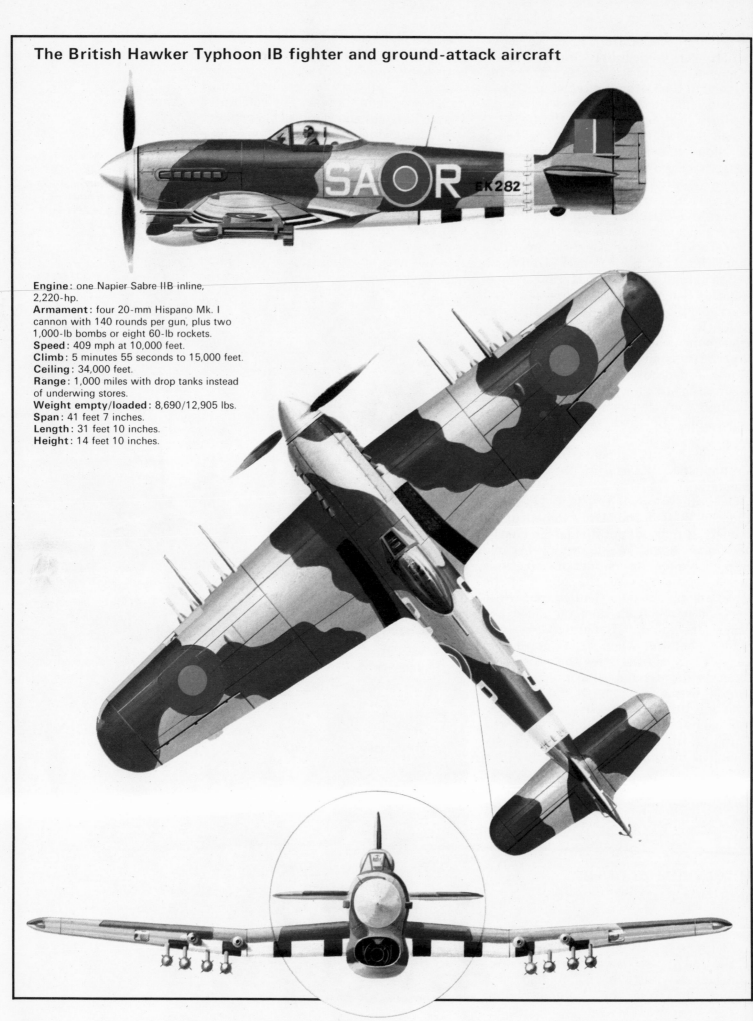

The British Hawker Typhoon IB fighter and ground-attack aircraft

Engine: one Napier Sabre IIB inline, 2,220-hp.
Armament: four 20-mm Hispano Mk. I cannon with 140 rounds per gun, plus two 1,000-lb bombs or eight 60-lb rockets.
Speed: 409 mph at 10,000 feet.
Climb: 5 minutes 55 seconds to 15,000 feet.
Ceiling: 34,000 feet.
Range: 1,000 miles with drop tanks instead of underwing stores.
Weight empty/loaded: 8,690/12,905 lbs.
Span: 41 feet 7 inches.
Length: 31 feet 10 inches.
Height: 14 feet 10 inches.

The American Lockheed P-38J Lightning long range fighter and fighter-bomber

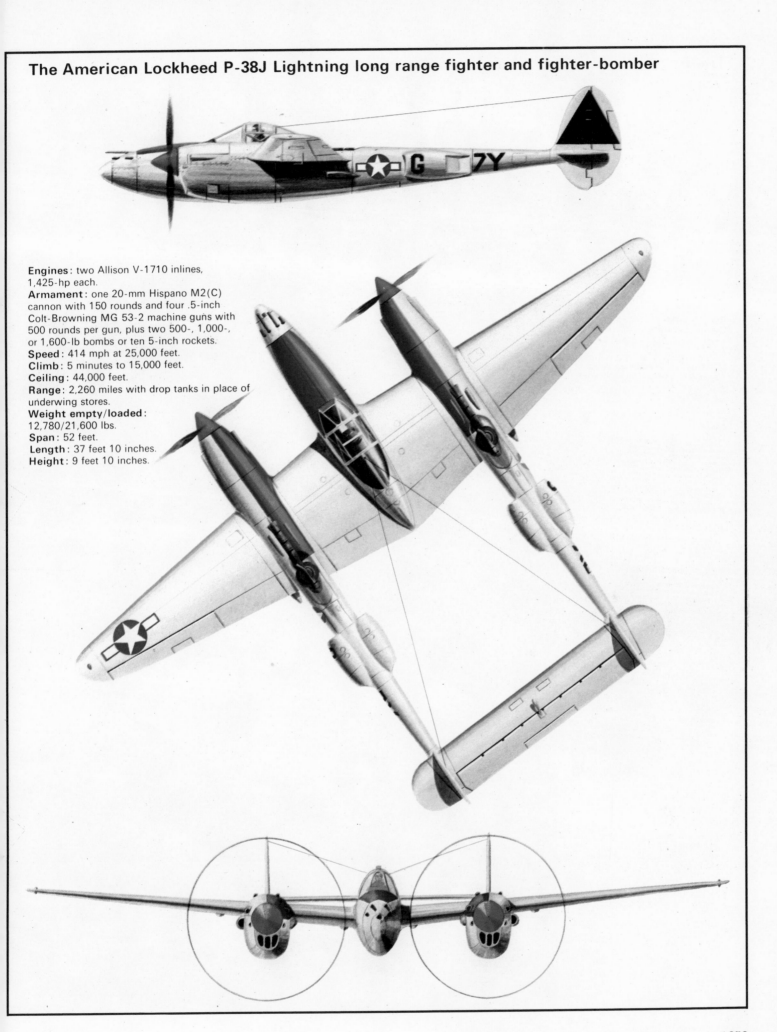

Engines: two Allison V-1710 inlines, 1,425-hp each.
Armament: one 20-mm Hispano M2(C) cannon with 150 rounds and four .5-inch Colt-Browning MG 53-2 machine guns with 500 rounds per gun, plus two 500-, 1,000-, or 1,600-lb bombs or ten 5-inch rockets.
Speed: 414 mph at 25,000 feet.
Climb: 5 minutes to 15,000 feet.
Ceiling: 44,000 feet.
Range: 2,260 miles with drop tanks in place of underwing stores.
Weight empty/loaded: 12,780/21,600 lbs.
Span: 52 feet.
Length: 37 feet 10 inches.
Height: 9 feet 10 inches.

△ △ *"Mulberry", the pre-fab port, in operation. Lorries on "Spud" pier-head.*
△ *A ticket home. Canadian wounded await embarkation.*
▷ *British armour probes inland.*

woods to the north lumbered a Tiger tank, which drove on to the road and proceeded right down the line of half-tracks 'brewing up' one vehicle after another. Behind these there was some incidental armour—a dozen tanks belonging to Regimental H.Q., the artillery observers and a reconnaissance troop. The Tiger destroyed them in quick succession, scorning the fire of one Cromwell, which saw its 75-mm shells bounce off the sides of the German tank even at the range of a few yards! Within a matter of minutes the road was an inferno with 25 armoured vehicles blazing—all the victims of this one lone Tiger."

While we do not want to undervalue Captain Wittmann's exploit (he was the tank's commander) we must point out that the Cromwell was very inadequately armed with a 75-mm gun and also had totally inadequate armour protection; for this reason the Desert Rats' morale suffered seriously for several weeks.

The British 2nd Army's defeat was fully compensated for on the same day by the fall of Carentan, whose defenders succumbed to the concentric thrust of the American 29th Division and 101st Airborne Division. The 17th S.S. *Panzergrenadier* Division *"Götz von Berlichingen"* (Lieutenant-General Ostermann) was alerted on June 7 at its stations at Thouars but arrived too late to prevent General Bradley's V and VII Corps from joining up. When it crossed the Loire it received the same treatment from the fighter-bombers as the Panzer-*"Lehr"* Division. The Anglo-Americans now had a continuous front between the Dives and Saint Marcouf.

Allied reinforcements

During the first days of battle the Germans had already lost 10,000 prisoners and 150 tanks. Even more important, Montgomery and Eisenhower were as aware as Rommel and Rundstedt that, contrary to expectations, the defenders were not getting reinforcements as quickly as the attackers.

From June 7 to 12 the British and Americans put in their floating reserves, which had sailed on the same day as the first echelon; these consisted of five infantry and three airborne divisions. The American V Corps was joined by the 9th and 20th Divisions; the British XXX

△ *Six days after D-Day and Churchill crosses the Channel to see for himself.*

▽ *Montgomery shows Churchill a map of the beach-head while General Dempsey of 2nd Army looks on.*

△ *Americans in Çarentan, the first major town captured in their sector.*

Corps by the 7th Armoured and the 49th Divisions; and the British I Corps by the 51st Highland Division, giving 15 divisions (eight American) out of a total of 37 stationed in the U.K.: 362,547 men, 54,186 vehicles, and about 102,000 tons of supplies landed in a week.

According to S.H.A.E.F.'s estimates, Montgomery was faced by 21 divisions on June 12. In fact, the defence was reinforced at the following rate:

June 6　21st Panzer Division
June 7　12th Panzer Division
June 8　Panzer-*"Lehr"* Division
June 9　353rd Panzer Division
June 11 17th S.S. *Panzergrenadier*
　　　　Division
June 12 2nd Panzer and 3rd
　　　　Parachute Divisions

Including the five divisions guarding the area between Cabourg and Mont Saint Michel on D-Day, *Panzergruppe* "West" and the German 7th Army had 12 divisions (including five armoured divisions) in the line; however, the 716th Division was only a cypher and the 352nd and 709th Divisions had been badly mauled. The Panzers went into the attack at random, always behind schedule, and under strength.

German communications disorganised

The air offensive against the French and Belgian railway networks broadly paid the dividends expected of it. This action continued, but from the night of June 5-6 it was made doubly successful by the intervention of the Resistance against the German communications in accordance with the "Green Plan" compiled by French Railways, while the "Tortoise Plan" drawn up by the French Post Office was carried out just as successfully against the occupying forces' telephone communications.

Pierre de Préval has listed 278 acts of sabotage carried out by the French Resistance from June 6 to September 15, 1944 in the department of Meurthe-et-Moselle, and the position was similar in the other departments. On the route from Montauban to the Normandy front, the *Waffen*-S.S. 2nd Panzer Division *"Das Reich"* (Lieutenant-General Lammerding) was harried by the Corrèze *maquis*; the terrible reprisals taken on the in-

habitants of Tulle and Oradour by this division to avenge these ambushes remain unforgotten.

From now on the delay in building up the German defence on the invasion front is perfectly understandable, as the combined action of the Anglo-American forces and the French Resistance networks was effectively assisted by Hitler's personal interventions in war operations.

Hitler's error

We have mentioned that when he was expecting the landing, the Führer had an intuition that Normandy might well be the invasion's objective. But he revised his view as soon as Eisenhower had launched Operation "Overlord". Plainly, he thought, he was faced with a diversionary manoeuvre aimed at making him lower his guard in the Pas-de-Calais. If he were to fall into the trap laid for him, the final thrust would be aimed at him in the sector he had unwisely uncovered... but he was not so stupid! Nevertheless on June 8 Major Hayn, LXXXIV Corps' chief Intelligence officer, was brought

△ On June 14 Charles de Gaulle crossed the Channel to tour the narrow strip of liberated France inside the beach-head. Here he gets an enthusiastic welcome from the people of Bayeux.
◁ A smile and a handshake from Montgomery.

△ *American Firefly tanks roll through a Normandy town.*
▷ *Looking south towards St. Lô –a deceptive vision of the Promised Land. Every hedgerow and ridge crossing the path of the Allied advance was a wasp's nest of German defences.*

a copy of U.S. VII Corps' battle orders which had been discovered on board a barge that had grounded near Isigny after its crew had been killed. This document, which was quite unnecessarily verbose, not only revealed General Collins's intentions, but also listed V Corps' and the British XXX Corps' objectives. The Americans' mission was to reach the Cotentin western coast as soon as possible, and then to change direction to the north and capture Cherbourg. Without delay this battle order was passed through the correct channels; 7th Army, Army Group "B", Supreme Command West, and O.K.W. Hitler, however, obstinately stuck to his opinion that this was a deceptive manoeuvre, and in support of his view he quoted the *Abwehr*'s summaries stating that just before the landing there were 60 or even 67 British and American divisions stationed in Britain. He never asked himself whether the real deception lay in simulating the existence of 30 divisions concentrated in Kent and ready to cross the English Channel at its narrowest point. At the front, on the other hand, where the Germans saw most of the Allied units they had previously met in Africa and Sicily (U.S. 1st and 9th Divisions, British 7th Armoured Division and 50th and 51st Divisions), they dismissed the idea of a second landing in the north of France. But nothing was done and Rommel was forbidden to use the 18 divisions of the 15th Army which, with the exception of the 346th and 711th Divisions, which were engaged on the right bank of the Orne, remained in reserve until after the breakthrough.

Rommel's plan abandoned

After a week's fighting, Rommel transmitted his appreciation and his intentions to Keitel: "The Army Group is endeavouring to replace the Panzer formations by infantry formations as soon as possible, and re-form mobile reserves with them. The Army Group intends to switch its *Schwerpunkt* in the next few days to the area Carentan–Montebourg to annihilate the enemy there and avert the danger to Cherbourg. Only when this has been done can the enemy between the Orne and the Vire be attacked."

The following conclusions can be drawn from this telephone message:

1. Rommel stated he was compelled to give up his first plan to push the enemy back into the sea immediately. Hitler therefore was not able to recover on the Western Front the forces which he hoped to collect to support the Eastern Front.
2. In order to release his armoured formations from the front, he would have had to have the same number of infantry formations at his disposal at the appropriate time. For this purpose the veto imposed on him by Hitler on taking troops from the 15th Army did not simplify matters.
3. Even if he had obtained these infantry formations, what he stated in any case shows that Montgomery's idea of free manoeuvre, which he put into practice in Normandy, was soundly and judiciously conceived.
4. Without these formations he could not displace Army Group "B"'s point of main effort from the Caen–Tilly-sur-Seulles area to the Carentan–Montebourg area, and therefore the "strong point" of Cherbourg was from now on virtually written off.

Churchill visits the Normandy front

Georges Blond has written:

"On Monday June 12 shortly after midday a D.U.K.W. landed at Courseulles and drove over the sand. A group of officers who had been looking at the D.U.K.W. through their field glasses for a few moments came forward quickly. A corpulent gentleman was sitting behind the driver, wearing a blue cap and smoking a cigar. As soon as the vehicle had stopped he asked the officers in a loud voice: 'How do I get down?' Just then a soldier hurried up carrying a small ladder. Churchill walked down it with all possible dignity. He shook hands with Montgomery who was standing in front of him in a leather jacket and a black beret, and then with the other officers, Field-Marshal Smuts, Field-Marshal Alan Brooke, and Rear-Admiral Sir Philip Vian, commander of the British Eastern Naval Task Force.

"He then went to his waiting jeep. The jeep started off."

On the same day, June 12, after dark, the first V-1 rockets were fired in the direction of London.

▽ *An American M7 trundles past a knocked-out* Pzkw *IV. Overleaf:* Beginning of the end in the Cotentin: German soldiers walk out to surrender, waving a Red Cross flag, in Cherbourg.

CHAPTER 119
Cherbourg falls

Rommel's pessimism in no way tempted him to give up at the military level. Quite the contrary: until the anti-Hitler conspiracy, to which he had become a party, put an end to the criminal power of the Führer and the National Socialist Party, the interests of his country demanded that he should defend the front with which he had been entrusted with all the resolution at his command. Otherwise, when, with the death of Hitler, peace was discussed at the conference table, the German representatives would be empty-handed, and would have to accept any conditions the victors chose to impose.

This explains the ferocity with which, for two months, the Normandy battles were fought, for Field-Marshal von Kluge, who had succeeded Rundstedt on July 3, and Rommel a fortnight later, seems, quite unexpectedly, to have had the same reasoning as his predecessor.

The attack on Cherbourg

According to the plan worked out by General Montgomery, the port of Cherbourg was the first objective of the American 1st Army, and especially of VII Corps, which, with the landing of the 90th and 91st Divisions, and the 2nd Armoured Division, had gradually been brought up to six divisions. On the German side, LXXXIV Panzer Corps had been taken over by General von Choltitz, following the death of General Marcks, killed by a fighter-bomber on leaving his command post at Saint Lô. "May I respectfully request you not to take too many risks. A change of command now would be most unfortunate." This remonstrance on the part of his chief-of-staff, just as Marcks was getting into his car to visit the front, brought forth the following reply: "You and your existence! *We* can die honourably, like soldiers; but our poor Fatherland . . ." A few seconds later he was dead, struck by a shell which cut through the femoral artery of the one leg left to him since the retreat in Russia in the winter of 1941-42.

To defend the Cotentin area, Choltitz had five divisions (the 77th, 91st, 243rd, 353rd, and 709th); however, in their ranks was a certain number of Soviet volunteers, recruited mainly in the Ukraine, in the Crimea, and in the valleys of the Caucasus, from a dozen different nationalities,

△ and △△ *Huge explosions wreck the harbour installations at Cherbourg. The extensive German demolitions effectively denied the Allies the use of the port; the main stream of supplies and reinforcements would still have to come in through the Mulberry port and over the beaches.*
▷ *After four years of German occupation, a French home in Cherbourg proudly flies the* tricolour.

Back on the defensive as the result of the failure of his counter-attacks, Rommel now had no illusions about the fate awaiting his forces, and on June 11 he spoke quite openly about it to Vice-Admiral Ruge, in whom, quite justifiably, he had full confidence. In his view, the best thing that Germany could do, given her situation, was to end the war now, before the territorial bargaining counters she still held were prised from her grasp. But Hitler did not see things that way, and in any case, none of Germany's enemies was willing to enter into any negotiations.

△ Infantry and armour push deeper into Cherbourg.
▷ Safety first. Lobbing a brace of grenades over a wall to cope with possible snipers.

and this incredible hotch-potch had scarcely made them better fighting units. As Lieutenant-General von Schlieben, commander of the 709th Division, who was fully aware of this, said: "How do you expect Russians, in German uniform, to fight well against Americans, in France?" His own division was made up of rather elderly troops (30- to 35-year-olds), and some of the artillerymen of the coastal batteries were over 40.

The first part of General Bradley's plan to capture his objective was to advance to the west coast of the Cotentin, and then turn north, making his columns converge on Cherbourg. The 90th Division, however, in its first engagement, got into such trouble in crossing the Douve that at one time the Allied command thought seriously of breaking it up, and distributing it amongst the other divisions. Finally, General Bradley merely replaced its commander with Major-General Landrum, who, however, was quite incapable of infusing any life into it, so badly had its morale been affected by its baptism of fire.

In happy contrast, on June 14 the American 9th Division, which had already distinguished itself in Tunisia, crushed enemy resistance, which had been favoured by the marshy terrain. Commanded by a resolute and skilful soldier, Major-General Manton Eddy, it advanced quickly along a line Pont l'Abbé–Saint Sauveur-le-Vicomte–Barneville, reaching the western coast of the Cotentin at dawn on June 15, and thus isolating to the north the 77th, 243rd, and 709th Divisions –or what was left of them. Then Lieutenant-General Collins's VII Corps, covered in the south by his two airborne divisions and his 91st Division, launched an assault on Cherbourg. On the right was the 4th Division, commanded by Major-General Barton, and on the left, the 79th Division (Major-General Ira Wyche), which had just landed, and the 9th Division. The latter had less than a day to wheel from west to north, with all its supplies and arms–a difficult military exercise which General Eddy accomplished brilliantly.

"Within 22 hours", wrote General Bradley, "he was expected to turn a force of 20,000 troops a full 90 degrees toward Cherbourg, evacuate his sick and wounded, lay wire, reconnoitre the ground, establish his boundaries, issue orders, relocate his ammunition and supply dumps, and then jump off in a fresh attack on a front nine miles wide. Eddy never even raised his eyebrows and when H-hour struck, he jumped off on time."

It is true that the German LXXXIV Corps had been very badly mauled, and that under the incessant attacks of the Anglo-American air force, Generals Hellmich and Stegmann, commanding the 77th and 243rd Divisions respectively, had been killed. However, the speed with which the 9th Division switched fronts enabled the remnants of the 77th Division, now under the command of Colonel Bacherer, to slip through the American forward posts and regain the German lines, having captured on the way 250 prisoners, 11 jeeps, and thousands of yards of telephone cable.

Meanwhile, on either side of Carentan, the American XIX Corps had entered the line, between the left wing of VII Corps and the right wing of V Corps. On the whole, General Bradley could consider himself satisfied with the situation, until, on June 19, a storm destroyed the artificial port being set up on "Omaha" Beach, and hundreds of landing craft and thousands of tons of supplies were lost; this, in turn, created a very difficult weapons shortage for the 1st Army, and

delayed the entry into the line of General Middleton's VIII Corps.

Schlieben rejects ultimatum

In spite of these difficulties, VII Corps succeeded in overcoming the resistance that Schlieben, with forces much too slender for the wide front he was holding, tried to put up, on Hitler's own orders, at Cherbourg. However, he refused to reply to General Collins's first call to surrender, couched in the following terms: "You and your troops have resisted stubbornly and gallantly, but you are in a hopeless situation. The moment has come for you to capitulate. Send your reply by radio, on a frequency of 1520 kilocycles, and show a white flag or fire white signal flares from the naval hospital or the Pasteur clinic. After that, send a staff officer under a flag of truce to the farmhouse on the road to Fort-du-Roule, to accept the terms of surrender."

Fort Roule, the key to this great port, had indeed just fallen to the Americans, and Fort Octeville, where Schlieben and Rear-Admiral Hennecke had taken

▽ *The last ditch: German snipers leave their nests to surrender.*
▽▽ *The P.O.W. count begins at Cherbourg. A G.I. is covering this "bag" of German prisoners with a .50-inch machine gun.*

The American/British Sherman Tankdozer

This was the basic Sherman gun tank fitted with an M1 or M1A1 dozer blade, for use in clearing rubble and filling in craters in the face of opposition and knocking down enemy emplacements. The need for such vehicles had been realised at Cassino, and Tankdozers proved invaluable in such operations as the clearing of Caen. Other bulldozer-type modifications were developed for cutting through the high hedgerows in which Normandy abounds.

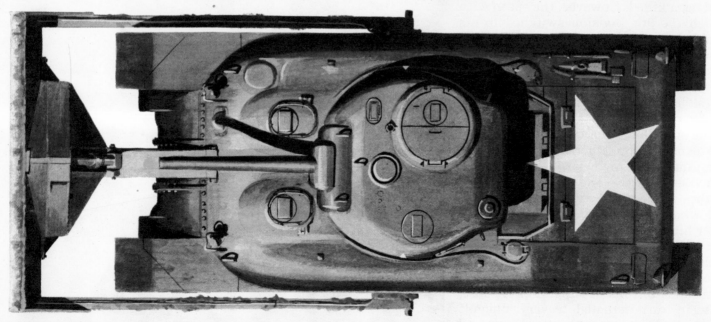

refuge, was being subjected to such an intense bombardment that clouds of poisonous fumes were seeping into the galleries where more than 300 wounded lay sheltering. This being so, Schlieben sent his negotiators to General Eddy on June 26, at 1400 hours, specifying that only Fort Octeville was to be discussed.

The time thus gained by the Germans enabled their pioneers to carry out the destruction of the port installations, and mine the ruins of the town, making the clearing up of the roads a longer and more costly process. In actual fact, only a month was needed before the Americans were able to bring in their first ships to Cherbourg; a few weeks later, an immense drum, 36 feet in diameter, was towed into Cherbourg harbour; around it were strung the last few yards of "Pluto" (Pipe Line Under The Ocean), the latest invention of Lord Louis Mountbatten, who had been responsible for the artificial port of Arromanches, which had resisted the storm of June 19 better than "Omaha". Starting at Sandown, on the Isle of Wight, Pluto's four tubes, each three inches in diameter and about 170 miles long, enabled 250,000 gallons of petrol a day to be pumped to the Allied armies.

The Allies occupy Cherbourg

The last strongholds of the town did not fall until July 3. On June 27, receiving the surrender of Major Küppers, Osteck fortress commander, General Barton, com-

△ △ *The "Battle of the Hedgerows"–a typical scene. Troops dash across a lane to reach cover on the far side. The tank in the foreground is a Panther.*
△ *Shermans squeeze past "killed" Panzers.*

manding the 4th Division, showed Küppers his map of the situation; later Küppers told Paul Carell:

"The entire network of the German positions was shown on the map with absolute accuracy, and in far greater detail than our own maps. On the back were listed precise data about the types of weapons and ammunition at each emplacement and bunker, as well as the names of all strongpoint commanders, and of the battalion and regimental commanders to whom they were responsible. The adjoining sheet covered the former defence sector 'East' in the Saint-Pierre-Eglise area outside the Cherbourg fortified zone . . . All command-posts showed the names of their principal officers. True, the entry for 11th Battery, 1709th Artillery Regiment still listed its commander Lieutenant Ralf Neste, who had lost his life in an accident with a *Panzerfaust* on May 5, 1944—but that seemed to be the only mistake.

"Their success had been tremendous. The full story of this gigantic espionage and Intelligence operation still remains to be written. It is the story of the Alliance of Animals, that most important secret Intelligence organization of the Allies in France; the story of 'Panther', the French Colonel Alamichel who set up the organisation; the story of Colonel Fay, who was known as 'Lion', and of Marie-Madeleine Merrie, that young, pretty, and courageous French woman who oddly enough bore the code-name of *Hérisson* ('Hedgehog').

▽ *Instant cavalry. Men of the U.S. 4th Division patrol Cherbourg on "liberated" horses.*

▷ *The shattered approaches to Cherbourg.*
▷ ▷ *"After the fight . . ." Amid a litter of abandoned German equipment, Sergeant Vernon Pickrell of Los Angeles samples a bottle of cognac found in a bunker.*

"The chief of the Alliance had three headquarters in Paris for the staff of officers and for his British chief radio-operator, 'Magpie'. One of these head-quarters was the contact point for couriers, the second was an alternative headquarters for emergencies, and the third, in the Rue Charles Laffitte, was headed by 'Odette', the famous Odette. At these headquarters all information converged. Here it was sorted according to Army, Navy, Air Force, political or economic."

Germans stand firm

But Bradley had no intention of resting on his laurels. He quickly brought his VII Corps into the line, in between the left wing of VIII Corps and the right wing of XIX Corps, such was his impatience to begin phase two of the Normandy campaign, which meant breaking up the German front between Saint Lô and Coutances, and then exploiting this breakthrough in the direction of Avranches. The operation had to be carried out quickly, so as to prevent the enemy digging in and returning to the techniques of trench warfare which had caused such bloody losses in 1914-18.

On June 24, Bradley's 1st Army consisted of VIII, VII, XIX and V Corps (nine infantry divisions, two armoured divisions, and the 82nd and 101st Airborne Divisions, although these latter were badly in need of a rest). His resources were thus greater than those of the enemy's 7th Army, but the Germans were tough, well commanded, and in good heart, as is shown by this letter, written by a German sergeant who had been taken prisoner: "The R.A.F. rules the skies. I have not yet seen a single plane with a 'swastika', and despite the material superiority of the enemy we Germans hold firm. The front at Caen holds. Every soldier on this front is hoping for a miracle and waits for the secret weapons which have been discussed so much."

In particular, between the sea and the Vire, in the sector where the American VII and VIII Corps were in action, the nature of the terrain favoured the defence, since both towards Coutances and Saint Lô marshy land alternated with wood-land. If the tanks took to the main roads, they fell victims to the redoubtable German 8.8-cm, which pounded them whilst

difficult; bad weather made air sorties, if not impossible, at least very dangerous, not least for the troops they were intended to support.

These different factors explain the slowness of the American advance across the swollen rivers and the flooded meadows of this neck of the Cotentin which extends between the Channel and the estuary of the River Vire. VIII Corps only took la Haye-du-Puits at the cost of exhausting combat; whilst VII Corps, despite the nickname "Lightning Joe" which they had bestowed on their dynamic General Collins, only became masters of what was left of the ruins of Saint Lô on July 20, 44 days later than laid down in the plan drawn up the April before . . . And not without quite considerable losses.

General Bradley, referring to this fierce resistance which halted his advance and cost so many lives, has given the following description of the ordeals his men had to undergo as they fought through Nor-

△ Tearing down the sign from the H.Q. of the hated Organisation Todt *at Cherbourg.*
▷ The German P.O.W. column moves out.

▽ On the Cherbourg battlefield: a captured German mortar.

remaining safely out of range; if they took to the little-used country roads, they got in everybody's way and at the same time exposed themselves to the risk of being shot at by a *Panzerschreck* or a *Panzerfaust* fired through a neighbouring hedge. Furthermore, the wet weather of the second half of June and the whole of July reduced to a minimum those air force sorties which could have helped the American 1st Army; even in fine weather the rolling green woodlands of the region would have made air support

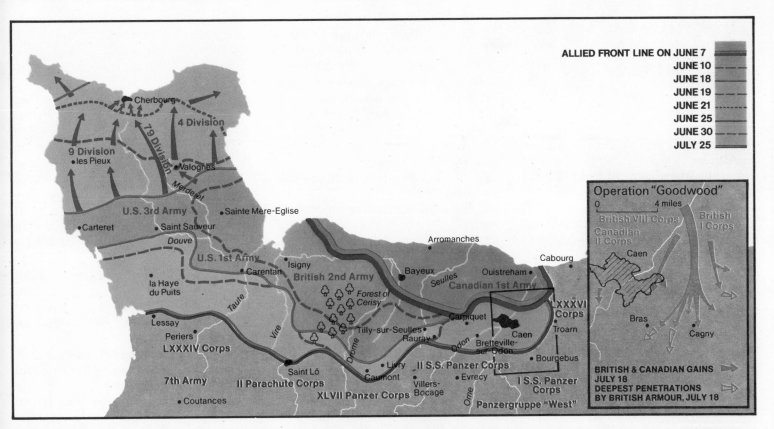

Operation "Goodwood"

0   4 miles

British VIII Corps
Canadian II Corps
British I Corps

Caen

Bras

Cagny

BRITISH & CANADIAN GAINS
JULY 18
DEEPEST PENETRATIONS
BY BRITISH ARMOUR, JULY 18

Cherbourg

4 Division

9 Division
les Pieux

79 Division

Valognes

Merderet

U.S. 3rd Army

Carteret

Saint Sauveur

Sainte Mère-Eglise

Douve

U.S. 1st Army

la Haye
du Puits

Isigny

Carentan

British 2nd Army

Bayeux

Arromanches

Seulles

Ouistreham

Cabourg

Canadian 1st Army

Forest of
Cerisy

Taute

Lessay

Periers

LXXXIV Corps

Vire

Tilly-sur-Seulles
Rauray

Carpiquet

Odon

Bretteville-
sur-Odon

Caen

LXXXVI
Corps

Troarn

Bourgebus

7th Army

Saint Lô

II Parachute Corps

Coutances

Douve

Livry

Caumont

Villers-
Bocage

XLVII Panzer Corps

Evrecy

II S.S. Panzer Corps

Ome

Panzergruppe "West"

I S.S. Panzer
Corps

mandy, Lorraine, the Ardennes, the Sieg-fried Line, and then into the very heart of Germany:

"The rifleman trudges into battle know-ing that statistics are stacked against his survival. He fights without promise of either reward or relief. Behind every river, there's another hill–and behind that hill, another river. After weeks or months in the line only a wound can offer him the comfort of safety, shelter, and a bed. Those who are left to fight, fight on, evading death but knowing that with each day of evasion they have exhausted one more chance for survival. Sooner or later, unless victory comes, the chase must end on the litter or in the grave."

And indeed, between June 22, the seventeenth day of the invasion, and July 19, American losses had leapt from 18,374 (including 3,012 dead), to 62,000, more precisely 10,641 dead and 51,387 wounded, two-thirds of whom, if not more, were as usual the long-suffering infantry-men.

These mounting losses and the very slow progress being made by the Ameri-can 1st Army provoked a fair amount of criticism from the host of correspondents accredited to S.H.A.E.F., especially as from June 22 the Russian summer offen-sive, with its almost daily victories, allowed unflattering comparisons to be made on Eisenhower and Bradley: com-pared with Vitebsk, Orcha, Mogilev, Bob-

ENTRE LE MARTEAU ...

... ET L´ENCLUME !..

ruysk, and Minsk, la Haye-du-Puits, Pont-Hébert, Tribehou, and even Saint Lô were but puny things. Some even went so far as to say that the "halting" of operations on the Western Front was part of some concerted plan, drawn up at the highest level, and intended to bleed the long-suffering Russians white with a view to the future.

△ *How the Allies consolidated the Normandy beach-head.*
◁ *Proud acknowledgment of the co-operation between the Anglo-American invasion forces and the work of the Resistance.*

1943

May

30. Churchill and de Gaulle arrive in Algiers.
Naval bombardment of Pantelleria.

June

1. Air offensive against Pantelleria augments the naval bombardment.
6. Second phase of air attack on Pantelleria.
11. British occupy Pantelleria after token resistance.
18. Wavell appointed Viceroy of India.
20. Italians order evacuation of Naples and Sicilian towns.

July

4. General Sikorski and other Polish leaders killed when their aircraft crashes.
5. Germans launch their last major offensive in the East in a move to pinch out the Kursk salient.
9. British airborne troops make landings in Sicily. Russian prepared defences bear the weight of the German attack at Kursk.
10. Main Allied landings in Sicily.
12. "The Greatest Tank Battle in History" fought near Prokhorovka as Russians swing onto the offensive.
14. Axis counter attacks in Sicily.
15. Russians launch offensive near Orel.
16. Churchill and Roosevelt call on Italians to surrender.
19. U.S.A.A.F. attacks Rome marshalling yards.
20. Italians surrender in western Sicily.
22. Americans capture Palermo.
24. King of Italy invited to command armed forces.
25. Mussolini resigns and is arrested.
26. Martial law in Italy; Fascist Party dissolved.
26-29. Air attacks on Hamburg leave 20,000 killed and 800,000 homeless.

August

1. Air attack on Ploieşti oil fields. 61 bombers lost, extensive but superficial damage to the target.
2. Hitler orders to hold in the East, but Manstein ignores him and fights a flexible defence in Khar'kov area.
6-7. Battle of Vella Gulf. Japanese lose three destroyers.

12. Large scale evacuation of Sicily by German forces.
14. Rome declared an open city.
14-24. "Quadrant" (First Quebec) Conference.
17. Americans enter Messina. R.A.F. bombs Peenemünde rocket research establishment.
22. Germans withdraw from Khar'kov.
25. Mountbatten appointed Supreme Commander, S.E. Asia.

September

3. 8th Army assault on Calabria. Armistice with Italy signed in secret, to become effective on the 8th.
6-9. Spitsbergen raid by *Tirpitz* and *Scharnhorst*.
9. Allied landings at Salerno. Kesselring moves quickly to isolate the area.
18. Climax of the Battle of Berlin. R.A.F. drops 350 4,000-lb bombs in half an hour.
20-24. Tarawa. In heavy fighting the U.S. Marines lose 985 killed and 2,193 wounded. Of the Japanese garrison 100 are taken prisoner, only 17 of them soldiers, out of a total of 4,700 men.
22. First Cairo Conference.
28-30. Teheran Conference. Stalin presented with Sword of Stalingrad, and told of Allied invasion plans for May or June 1944.

October

2. Luftwaffe raid on Bari hits ammunition ships.
3. Russians advance on a wide front.
3-7. Second Cairo Conference.
5. Long range P-51 fighters begin escorting daylight raids.

7. 8th Army makes unsuccessful attack on Ortona.

8. General Spaatz to command U.S. Strategic Air Forces in Europe.

12. Czech-Soviet alliance signed in Moscow. Rommel appointed C.-in-C. Fortress Europe.

14. Russians open winter offensive.

15. Germans accused of atrocities are tried at Khar'kov.

17. 5th Army takes San Pietro.

21. Russians destroy German bridge-head.

24. Roosevelt announces the names of the commanders of the European liberation forces.

24-26. The last cruise of the *Scharnhorst*. Only 36 of her 1,900 complement are rescued.

26. Russians launch new offensive on Kiev salient. U.S. Marines land at Cape Gloucester.

29. Marines secure Cape Gloucester airfield.

10-14. Struggle for the beach-head.

12. Skorzeny rescues Mussolini.

17-18. Kesselring gives Vietinghoff permission to evacuate Salerno area.

20. Union of German officers in Russia calls for a coup against Hitler.

21-22. British midget submarines attack the *Tirpitz* in Altenfjord.

25. Russians take Smolensk.

27. 8th Army takes Foggia.

29. Badoglio signs armistice terms.

November

1. 5th Army captures Naples. Averell Harriman appointed U.S. Ambassador to Moscow.

4. Cunningham becomes First Sea Lord.

6. Americans land on Kolombangara Island.

7. 5th Army halted at Volturno defences.

13. Italy declares war on Germany. Allies cross the Volturno.

14. Schweinfurt raid. 8th Air Force attacks German ball-bearing industry. 62 aircraft lost and 138 damaged. Americans halt long range unescorted raids.

19-30. Moscow Conference. Allied foreign ministers prepare for the Teheran Conference.

21. Subhas Chandra Bose announces formation of Govern-

ment of Free India in Singapore.

23. Melitopol' liberated.

December

2. Battle of Empress Augusta Bay. Japanese lose one cruiser and one destroyer.

6. Russians recapture Kiev.

8. 8th Army gains the Sangro heights.

1944

January

1. General Mark Clark takes command of U.S. 7th Army, and retains command of the 5th.

5. 5th Army begins final assault on the Winter Line.

8. Trial of Ciano, de Bono, and other Fascists at Verona.

15. 5th Army takes Monte Trocchio. Germans withdraw across the Rapido. Russians open offensives for Leningrad and Novgorod.

16. Eisenhower assumes duties as Supreme Commander, Allied Expeditionary Forces.

19. Russians take Novgorod.

20. Americans reach the Rapido. Air Chief-Marshal Sir Arthur Tedder becomes Deputy Supreme Commander, Allied Expeditionary Forces.

22. Anzio landings, 50,000 men and 5,200 vehicles under General Lucas.

26. Russians publish their own report on the Katyn Wood murders.

27. Leningrad relieved.

29. The Battle of Korsun' begins.

30. 5th Army breaks into the Gustav Line.

February

4-12. Japanese counter-attack in the Arakan.

5. Chindit 16th Brigade begins move toward Indaw.

6. Russians trap five German divisions in Nikopol' area.

8. "Overlord" plans confirmed. 5th Army reaches Monastery Hill at Cassino.

13-25. With air dropped supplies British counter-attack in Arakan.

15. Air and artillery bombardment destroys Cassino Abbey. New Zealanders and Indians begin offensive to clear heights.

16. U.S. task force begins strikes against Truk in the Carolines.

18. Truk airfields wrecked. 200,000 tons of merchant shipping, one cruiser and one destroyer sunk. R.A.F. bombs Amiens prison in Operation "Jericho".

19. U.S. troops land on Eniwetok Atoll.

20-26. The "Big Week". In five days the British and American bomber forces strike in co-ordinated attacks by day and night.

23. Lucas relieved of command at Anzio and replaced by General L. K. Truscott Jr. German counterattacks drive back the forward Allied elements.

24. Russians overrun Dno, Rogachev.

25. British clear Japanese from Ngakyedyauk Pass in Burma.

29. U.S. Army troops land on Admiralty Islands, seize airstrip on Los Negros.

March

1. Russians launch new offensive in the north across Narva river. Sauckel admits that of 5,000,000 foreign workers in Germany only 200,000 are volunteers. Chindit 16th Brigade crosses Chindwin.

4. First raid on Berlin by U.S.A.A.F.

5. Chindits land on Broadway and Piccadilly strips north-east of Indaw.

9. Japanese attack on Bougainville.

15. Preceded by heavy air support, New Zealanders and Indians attack Cassino.

17. British blow up Manipur bridge in Kohima-Imphal region. New Zealanders break through at Cassino and take railway station.

25. Wingate killed in air crash, replaced by Major General W. D. A. Lentaigne.

28. Nikolayev falls to the Russians.

29. Siege of Imphal begins.

April

3. Carrier-based bombers hit the *Tirpitz* in a surprise raid killing 300 of the crew.

7. Goebbels appointed administrator of Berlin.

10. Odessa falls to the Red Army.

13. Red Army captures Feodosiya, Simferopol'.

16. Yalta captured by Soviet Independent Coastal Army.

22. Americans make unopposed landing at Hollandia, Dutch New Guinea.

29. 120 aircraft destroyed in two day strike on Truk Atoll by Task Force 58.

May

5. 14th Army begins attack on Assam. Japanese announce the death of Admiral Koga.

7. Russians begin attack on Sevastopol'.

9. Sevastopol' taken by Russians. Allied air forces begin large-scale attacks on French airfields in preparation for D-Day.

11. 5th and 8th Armies open offensive on the Gustav Line.

12. Allies cross Garigliano, Rapido rivers. Last German forces evacuated from Crimea.

13. Allies take St. Angelo, Castelforte, and open the way to Rome.

15. Germans begin to withdraw from the Gustav Line.

16. Last Japanese troops cleared from Kohima Ridge.

18. Poles capture Cassino monastery.

23. Allied break-out from Anzio beach-head.

25. Troops from Anzio link up with 5th Army patrols at Terracina.

27. Americans land on Biak Island.

29. First tank battle of South West Pacific is fought on Biak.

June

2. General Alexander calls on the citizens of Rome to save their city from destruction.

3. Hitler authorises Kesselring to withdraw from Rome. End of the battle of Kohima.

4. 5th Army enters Rome.

5. Airborne troops drop at night in Normandy.

6. D-Day. Allied naval forces land troops on beaches between Cherbourg and Le Havre. 7,500 sorties flown by 0800 hours. 176,000 troops land with their *matériel*, by nightfall five divisions are ashore.

7. Allies reach Bayeux and clear beach-heads.

8. U.S. forces reach Eniwetok and Kwajalein.

9. St. Mère-Eglise and Trevières liberated. Allied aircraft begin operating from French airstrips. German counter-attack fails.

10. Montgomery establishes H.Q. in Normandy.

12. All the Normandy bridgeheads linked, front extends to 50 miles.

13. First V-1's begin to fall on England.